CW01645768

A QUICK COURSE IN

WINDOWS 3.1

SALLEY OBERLIN

PATRICK KERVRAN

JOYCE COX

AN ONLINE PRESS BOOK

PUBLISHED BY
Online Press Incorporated
14320 NE 21st Street, Suite 18
Bellevue, WA 98007 (800) 854-3344

Publisher's Cataloging in Publication
(prepared by Quality Books Inc.)

Oberlin, Salley, 1948–
A quick course in windows 3.1 / Salley B. Oberlin, Patrick Kervran, Joyce Cox.
p. cm.
Includes index.
ISBN 1-879399-14-8

1. Windows (Computer programs) I. Kervran, Patrick J., 1961–. II. Cox, Joyce K., 1946– III. Title. IV. Title: Windows 3.1.

QA76.76.W56O2 1992 005.4'3
QBI92-121
92-60030
CIP

Printed and bound in the United States of America

1 2 3 4 5 6 7 8 9 O W O L 3 2 1 0

Distributed to bookstores by Publishers Group West, (800) 788-3123

Contents

Introduction

For a number of years now, we've been answering questions about computers and software. Each time we've helped a bewildered and sometimes desperate person learn a new procedure, we've wondered why people don't use the product documentation or read any of the available computer books. Linda is a store manager; Ted is a school teacher; Barbara works in a law firm; John is a quality-control specialist. They are all educated and astute; they are all used to planning their time, setting goals, and making decisions. So what do they all have in common? They are all very busy!

The people who come to us have more important things to do than wade through page after page of software documentation or digest a 300-page computer book. They all want fast answers and straightforward, easy-to-follow instructions on how to complete the task at hand. They aren't interested in a lot of background information or in learning two approaches to the same task—they just want to get the job done.

If you're a busy person who wants to know how to integrate Microsoft Windows into your work life, we think you'll find that *A Quick Course in Windows 3.1* is just what you've been looking for. In this book, we cover loading Windows, organizing files in a logical fashion for easy retrieval, switching among Windows and non-Windows applications, and sharing information. We show you how to perform everyday tasks and create real-life documents with Windows' wide range of accessories. We deliberately focus on what you might want to do with Windows, not on what Windows does.

Because not everyone learns in the same way, all *Quick Course*™ books offer a varied learning approach. For the person who simply wants to perform the task at hand, we offer no-nonsense, to-the-point guidance. For the person who wants additional information about program concepts, shortcuts, jargon, pitfalls, and so on, we have placed shaded boxes throughout the book that offer deeper insights into some of the topics at hand. Like all *Quick Course*™ books, this book also has a special binding that allows it to lay flat on your desk, so you can read it easily while you work at your computer.

There's a well-known saying in the computer industry that 80 percent of the people who buy best-selling software products use only 20 percent of the products' features. What we offer is streamlined instruction for the new user. Because Windows makes *using* the computer quick and easy, we think *learning* Windows should be quick and easy. It is not our intention to describe every command and feature of the program—the manual does that. Instead, we cover only what you need to know to begin using Windows effectively. You can read this book in less than a day and work through the examples in just a few hours. Our goal is to help you integrate Windows into your daily work life with as little fuss as possible.

Enough said. It's time to put Windows to work.

1

What's the Big Deal About Windows?

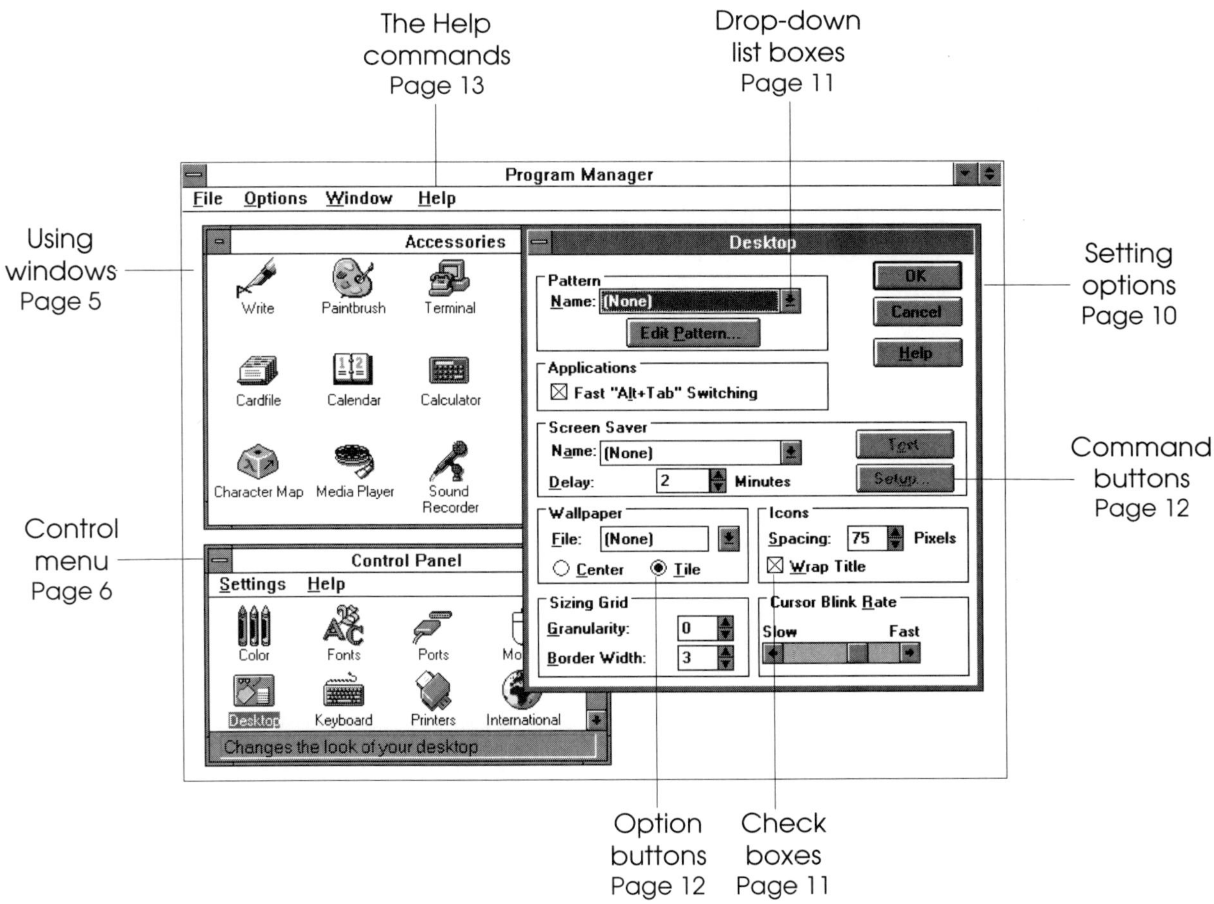

The Help commands Page 13
Drop-down list boxes Page 11
Using windows Page 5
Setting options Page 10
Command buttons Page 12
Control menu Page 6
Option buttons Page 12
Check boxes Page 11
Program Manager
File Options Window Help
Accessories
Write
Paintbrush
Terminal
Cardfile
Calendar
Calculator
Character Map
Media Player
Sound Recorder
Control Panel
Settings Help
Color
Fonts
Ports
Desktop
Keyboard
Printers
International
Changes the look of your desktop
Desktop
Pattern
Name: (None)
Edit Pattern...
OK
Cancel
Help
Applications
Fast "Alt+Tab" Switching
Screen Saver
Name: (None)
Delay: 2 Minutes
Test
Setup...
Wallpaper
File: (None)
Center
Tile
Icons
Spacing: 75 Pixels
Wrap Title
Sizing Grid
Granularity: 0
Border Width: 3
Cursor Blink Rate
Slow
Fast

Microsoft Windows has been a topic of conversation for well over a year now—long enough for even the skeptics to realize that it is not just a flash in the pan. People who formerly showed little interest in computers have been won over by the convenience of the Windows graphical environment. Computer magazines that were quick to analyze the impact of Windows version 3.0 were equally quick to pump out articles about the latest version, Windows 3.1.

Why all the fuss? What makes Windows so special? In this chapter we discuss Windows' main claims to fame. We also describe some of the features of Windows that make using your computer easier and more intuitive than ever before, which in turn helps you to be more productive. If you are a recent convert from the Apple Macintosh, or if you are otherwise familiar with the features of graphical interfaces, you might want to just skim this chapter.

A New Way to Communicate

Graphical user interface

Windows provides an environment, called a *graphical user interface*, that allows you to communicate visually with your computer. With Windows, you no longer have to remember obscure commands and type them at a DOS prompt to make the program work. You simply click a picture called an *icon* or select a command from a list called a *menu* to tell Windows what you want it to do.

Windows components

Windows is not just one program but a collection of utilities that creates a complete working environment. To get you oriented, you will find in the tip boxes on this and the facing page brief descriptions of some of the main Windows components.

Program Manager: the organizer

Program Manager is loaded automatically when you start Windows. In Program Manager, you use windows and icons to visually organize your programs into logical groups. You can also run programs directly from the Program Manager screen.

File Manager: the filing clerk

File Manager is a powerful hard-disk organizational aid that displays your directories as "tree" diagrams so that you can see how they are organized. It also gives you access to a wide selection of file-management tools.

It is important to understand that Windows is not an operating system like DOS. (The operating system's job is to handle communications between the program you are running and the hardware and software that are actually doing the work.) Windows is like any other program; you cannot run Windows without DOS. Windows' job resembles that of a translator. You use the Windows environment to give simple visual instructions which Windows then translates into a more complex language that DOS and the computer can understand.

Visual instructions

Graphical user interfaces (GUIs) are not new. The Apple Macintosh, which, because of its interface, took the computing world by storm when it was released in 1984, was just one of a series of systems that have used a visual "language" for people/computer communication. However, Windows is the first graphical environment for the huge IBM PC family that has gained support in the software industry.

Easy Transfer of Information

Windows makes it easier than ever before to transfer information from one program to another. Need a logo for your letterhead? You can create one with a paint program, copy it into a temporary storage area called the *Clipboard*, and then paste it into a word-processing document—in three easy steps. Because Windows allows you to run the paint program and the word-processing program simultaneously, moving

Clipboard

Clipboard: the temporary storage place

When you copy or move information from one place to another, it is temporarily stored in an area of memory called the Clipboard. You can view information that is stored on the Clipboard by displaying Clipboard Viewer (see page 34), but you can't change the information there.

Control Panel: the system customizer

You can control how Windows runs and looks by using the Control Panel utilities. In the Control Panel, you can specify fonts, colors, desktop patterns, icon spacing, mouse and keyboard speed, and other options allowing you to set up Windows so that it is comfortable and convenient to use.

Print Manager: the print queue monitor

Without Windows, some programs tie up your computer as they format and send pages to the printer. Print Manager works with all Windows programs to print documents while you keep working. Documents sent to Print Manager are queued and printed in order. You can reorganize or even delete print jobs from the queue to suit your needs.

from one program to the other is a simple matter of clicking a mouse button to switch between windows.

Multitasking

Called *multitasking*, running two or more programs concurrently saves you time by allowing you to keep all the information you need at your fingertips, whether it is stored in a report, a spreadsheet, a database, or any other type of file. If you're in the middle of writing a letter and need to look up some figures in a spreadsheet, you no longer have to stop what you are doing, quit the word processor, load the spreadsheet, find the figures, and then start your word processor again. You can simply flip between windows to get the information you need—in only a couple of easy steps.

The Visual Language of Windows

Some of the terms you'll learn as a Windows user might be new to you. Before we get started with the program, let's make sure we are all speaking the same language.

The Mouse

Some veteran PC users are convinced that Windows is part of a grand plot to make them use a mouse, and there is no question that working with Windows is a lot easier with one. Once you learn how to use a mouse proficiently, you'll use it as often as you use the keyboard. Using the mouse to pull

Pointing

Moving the mouse around on your desktop moves the pointer on your screen. To point to an item, simply move the mouse so that the pointer rests directly over that item.

Clicking

You click the mouse button to activate icons and windows, to resize windows, and to open menus. You also click options to select them. Clicking is simply a matter of pressing and releasing the left mouse button once. You also click to activate an insertion point in text so that you can make changes. This is called *clicking an insertion point.*

Double-clicking

You double-click the mouse button to start programs and open windows. Double-clicking works the same as clicking, except that you *quickly* click the mouse button twice. If you find that you can't double-click quickly enough, you can reset the double-click speed using the Mouse options in the Windows Control Panel.

down menus, select commands, scroll through windows, and so forth is much easier than performing the same operations with the keyboard. (We discuss all these operations in more detail later in the book.) Of course, you'll still use the keyboard to type text.

The Pointer

The pointer is a symbol on the screen that represents the movements you make with your mouse when you work. The pointer is usually an arrow, but it can take the form of a hand (when using Help), a text cursor (in a word processor), or an hourglass (when Windows is processing information). In a paint program such as Windows Paintbrush, the pointer changes shape with each tool you use; for example, it might take the shape of a pencil or a paint roller.

Windows

Windows are rectangular portions of the screen in which you view a group of icons that represent programs, other windows, or the contents of a file. Except when you are using a non-Windows application, everything you see in Windows is in a window.

All windows have a title bar, a frame, and a menu bar. A window might also have buttons and scroll bars. On the following pages, we'll look at each of these in more detail.

Dragging

Dragging repositions an icon or a window on the screen and resizes windows. Start by pointing at the item you want to drag. Then click it, and hold down the mouse button while moving the item. An outline of the icon or window frame follows the pointer. Release the button when the image is where you want it. The icon or window then moves to the new position.

Selecting characters

You identify text you want to cut, copy, or format by selecting it. Selecting text characters is probably the most difficult thing you'll have to do with your mouse. Click to the left of the first character you want to select, drag the mouse to the right of the last character, and then release the mouse button. You can also drag upward or downward to select entire lines at once. The selected text is displayed in reverse video, with the letters appearing light in color, and the selection bar appearing dark. You can then cut, copy, or format the text.

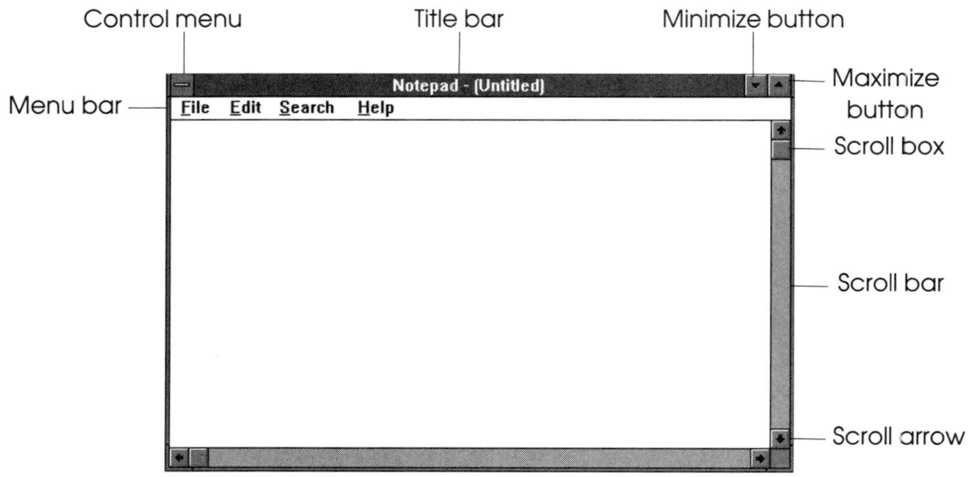

The Title Bar At the top of every window is a title bar that describes the function of the window or shows the name of the program or document displayed in it. When a window is active (meaning any tasks you perform take place in that window), its title bar is dark in color, indicating that the next action you perform will affect that window. When a window is not active, its title bar is light in color.

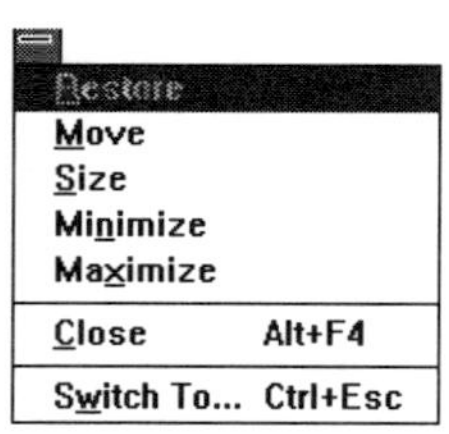

At the left end of every title bar is at least one menu: the Control menu. Those of you who are not used to a mouse can choose commands from the Control menu to carry out actions such as moving and resizing windows, closing windows, and switching between open documents. You can also use the Control menu to switch among open applications. The Control menu is available in every window, and it also appears in some dialog boxes (a topic we discuss on page 10).

To complicate matters, some applications allow you to open multiple document windows, each with its own title bar and Control menu, in addition to the application window's title bar and Control menu. However, the functions performed by the commands on these Control menus are fairly consistent from one application to another.

The Window Frame Except for some very simple programs like Calculator, all application and document windows have frames. Most frames can stretch and shrink to make their windows larger or smaller. As you move the pointer over different parts of a frame that is resizable, the pointer becomes

Resizing windows

a double-headed arrow, indicating the directions in which you can drag the frame to change its size. Drag the sides of the frame to the left and right, drag the top and bottom of the frame up and down, and drag the corners up and down diagonally. A window's frame disappears when you maximize the window.

The Menu Bar Across the top of every window is a menu bar, which shows the menus available for use with the items displayed in that particular window. A menu is a list of commands that carry out related tasks.

The Buttons Many windows have buttons in their title bars that are used to resize the window. The buttons have arrows on them to symbolize the function they perform. For example, at the right end of a window's title bar, you might find one or two arrows that enable you to resize the window quickly. Clicking the Minimize button (the downward-pointing arrow) shrinks the window down to an icon. Minimizing a window is a quick means of tucking the window out of the way without quitting the application or closing the file currently in the window. Clicking the Maximize button (the upward-pointing arrow) expands the window to the size of the full screen. Maximizing a window gives you a larger working space when you are running an application, but obscures any other windows. The Restore button (a double-headed arrow) appears only on maximized windows in place of the Maximize button to allow you to quickly return the maximized window to its previous size. Minimize, Maximize, and Restore also appear as commands on a window's Control menu. These commands duplicate the action of the buttons.

Shrinking windows

Expanding windows

The Scroll Bars Even when maximized, windows are often not big enough to display all of their contents, particularly if the file you have loaded is a long document or a large spread-sheet. For example, in Program Manager a window can contain more icons than are initially displayed. If there is more information in a window than can fit on one screen, scroll bars appear to help bring other parts of the screen into view. Windows can have scroll bars on their bottom and right sides, depending on how much of the window is out of view. You use the right scroll bar to move the contents up and down in the window and the bottom scroll bar to move the contents from side to side.

Scrolling a line

Scrolling a windowful

Learning to manipulate the scroll bars is crucial to working with Windows. You can use several different scrolling methods. Clicking the arrow at either end of a scroll bar moves the window's contents a line or a column at a time, whereas clicking on either side of the box in a scroll bar moves the contents a windowful at a time. You can also drag a scroll box to a new position in the scroll bar. In some windows, dragging the scroll box continuously scrolls the contents of the window, whereas in others the contents "snap" into place after you stop dragging the scroll box and release the mouse button. The position of the scroll box in relation to the scroll bar roughly indicates the position of the window in relation to its contents. For example, when the scroll box is in the middle of the scroll bar, the window is positioned roughly halfway through its contents.

Icons

An icon is simply a symbol. With Windows, icons are used to represent all sorts of items, including application programs (such as Word for Windows), documents, windows, and even commands. If you are working on a network, you might see an icon for your network server. To make using Windows as intuitive as possible, icons are usually easy to associate

Windows icons vs. Mac icons

If you are converting to Windows from the Macintosh, your mouse and window-handling skills will come in handy in the Windows environment. But toss out any preconceived ideas about icons! Icons in the Windows environment bear no real relationship to the files they represent. For example, deleting a program icon in Program Manager doesn't delete the program; it simply deletes the icon! Similarly, duplicating an icon doesn't duplicate the document or program it represents; it simply makes a copy of the icon.

with the item they represent. For example, the icon for Terminal, the Windows telecommunications program, is a telephone sitting on a modem. In case the symbol is not instantly recognizable, each icon has a name. When you select an icon in order to do something with it (such as move it), its name is highlighted.

Terminal

The Desktop

The Windows background screen, on which all windows and icons appear, is known as the *desktop*. This well-worn metaphor is designed to make using the tools available with Windows no more intimidating than using the familiar tools found on a typical desk in a typical office.

One Windows program, Program Manager, always appears on the desktop, either as an icon or a window. If you want to jazz up your desktop, you can use the Windows Control Panel to change the color and pattern of the background (see page 108 for more information about the Control Panel). You can even use a graphic as desktop "wallpaper." But be forewarned: Icons may not show up very well against complex illustrations.

Menus and Commands

To carry out most tasks, you need to choose commands from menus. In the menu bar, click the name of the menu you want. The menu drops down, displaying a list of commands. To choose a command, click the command name.

Choosing commands with the keyboard

If you find it quicker to use the keyboard, you can activate the menu bar by pressing Alt and then open the menu by typing the underlined letter in the menu name. You can then choose a command by typing the underlined letter in the command name. Once you learn the letters for menus and commands, you can type the key sequence quickly to choose the command. For example, to exit Program Manager (and exit Windows), you can type Alt+F+X.

Some command names are displayed in "gray" letters, indicating that you can't choose those commands at this time. For example, the Maximize command appears in gray when the window is already maximized.

Some command names are followed by an ellipsis (...), indicating that you must supply more information in a special kind of window called a *dialog box* before the command can be carried out.

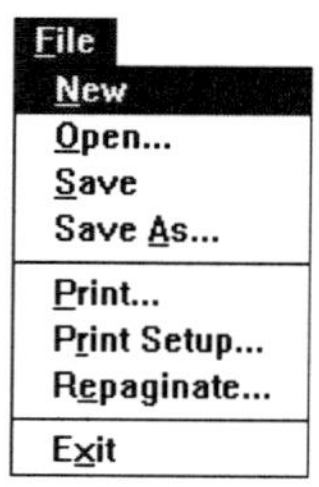

As part of the effort to give all Windows applications a common look, menus with commands that carry out similar tasks often have the same names in different applications. The Control menu, File menu, Window menu, and Help menu are examples of common menus. In all likelihood, the File menu will be the menu you use most often. This menu usually contains commands such as New (for creating new windows or documents), Open (for opening windows or documents), Save (for saving the current document), and Exit (to leave the current program, or to leave Windows).

Dialog Boxes

Dialog boxes are Windows' way of allowing you to give information or to select from several different options so that a particular command can be carried out. Here's a typical dialog box:

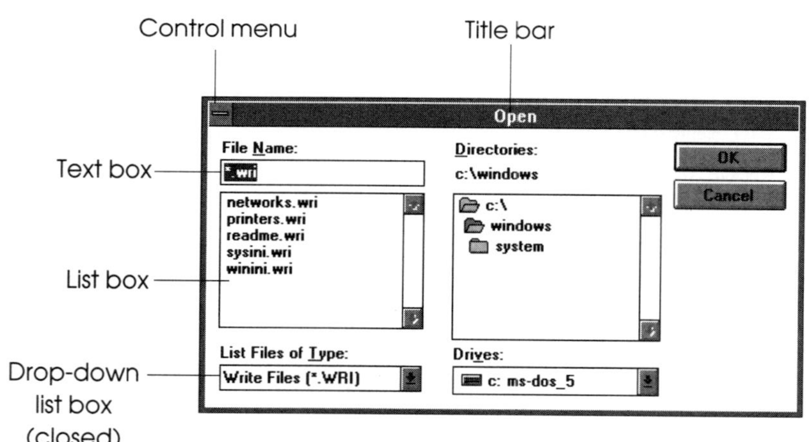

At the top of the next page is a more complex dialog box.

You usually give information by typing it in a text box. You select an option by highlighting the option you want in a list box or drop-down list box, or by clicking a check box or option button. You use command buttons, such as Cancel and OK, to confirm your selections or give other instructions.

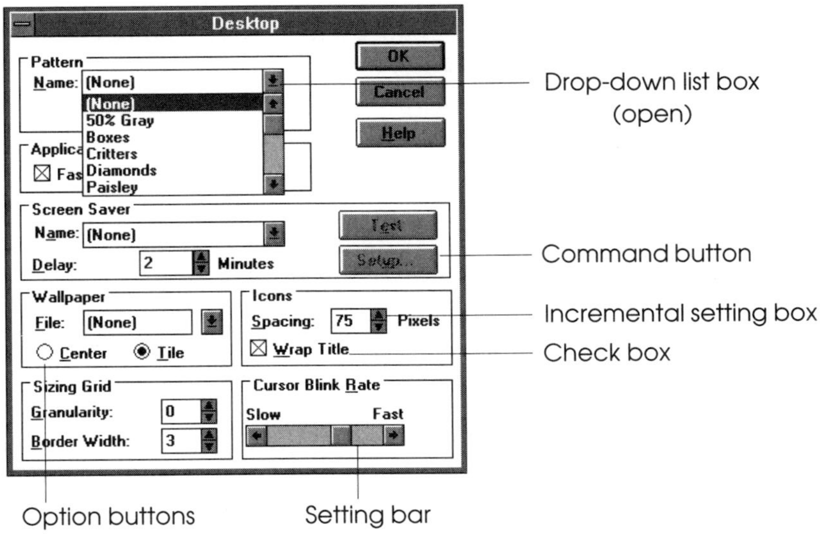

List Boxes A list box displays a series of choices that will vary from computer to computer. Generally, Windows uses a list box to display the names of available documents. The list box usually has a text box associated with it. You enter a selection in the text box by clicking an item in the list box, which highlights the item, or by typing the item directly in the text box.

Scrollable list boxes

When more choices are available than can fit in the list box, they are displayed in a list box equipped with scroll bars. You scroll the list in the same way you scroll a window: Simply click the arrow at either end of the scroll bar. In most scrolling lists, dragging the scroll box continuously scrolls the list; in many lists, typing a letter in the text box scrolls the list to the choices that begin with the letter you typed.

Drop-Down List Boxes Initially, a drop-down list appears in the dialog box as a box containing an option. To the right of the box is a downward-pointing arrow, which indicates that other options are available if the one displayed doesn't meet your needs. Clicking the arrow drops down a list of the other options. To select another option, you simply click it. Drop-down list boxes with many options often have scroll bars, which you use just like those in scrolling lists.

Check Boxes Check boxes are small squares. Clicking an empty check box selects the associated option; an *X* appears in the box to indicate that the option is active, or turned on.

Clicking the box again removes the *X* to indicate that the option is inactive, or turned off. Check boxes operate independently of one another, so from a group of check boxes you can select none, one, or all of the options, as required for the task at hand.

Option Buttons Option buttons are round, and they always appear in a group of mutually exclusive options. When you click an option button, a black dot appears in the button to indicate that the option is active. Because only one of the group of buttons can be active at a time, the black dot disappears from the button of the previously active option.

Text Boxes As we've said, you enter variable information, such as filenames, in a dialog box by typing it in a text box. If the text box already contains an entry and you want to replace it, you highlight the text (if it isn't already highlighted) and then simply overtype the old text with the new. You can double-click the text box to select the text quickly.

Command Buttons Most dialog boxes have at least two command buttons, OK and Cancel. Clicking OK closes the dialog box and carries out the command according to your specifications. Clicking Cancel closes the dialog box and also cancels the command. The buttons usually have a shaded, three-dimensional look and appear "pressed" when you click them. One command button usually has a heavy border around it to indicate that pressing Enter selects that button.

Direct access to other dialog boxes

Some dialog boxes have additional command buttons, which you can use to refine the original command. If the label on a button is followed by an ellipsis (...), clicking the button opens another dialog box. You select options in this second dialog box in the usual way. Clicking OK or Cancel closes the second box and returns you to the first box.

Warning Messages Windows applications display messages and warnings in dialog boxes when a command can't be carried out or when there is a chance you might regret having chosen the command—for example, when deleting files. Here's a typical warning:

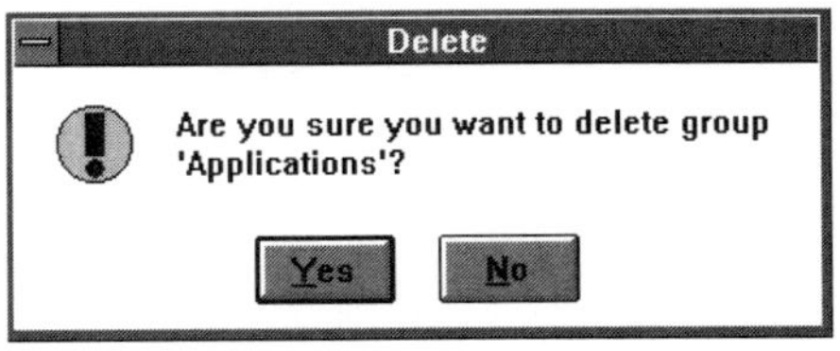

Clicking Cancel or No cancels the command and closes the warning dialog box, whereas clicking OK or Yes acknowledges the message and continues the command.

Getting Help

Using Windows is fairly intuitive, and this book will help you find your way around so that, most of the time, you will know exactly what to do and how. However, for those times when you stumble over a particular operation, Windows provides an excellent Help feature. Think of the Help feature as an encyclopedia-sized book that you can page through for help. Windows provides Help files for all its programs, and most other Windows applications provide them as well.

An overview of Help topics

A full program in its own right, Help can be accessed by choosing a topic from the Help menu that appears in most Windows applications. In addition, a Help button appears in many dialog boxes. Usually, the Help menu has an Index or Contents command that gives you a broad view of the Help topics available for that application. Here is the window you see when you choose Contents from Program Manager's Help menu:

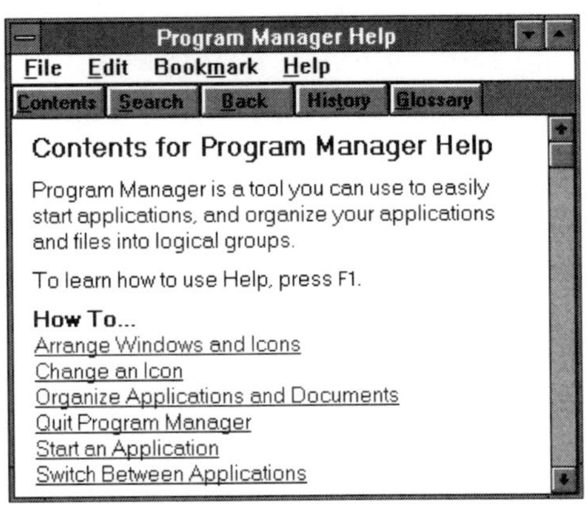

Other commands on the Help menu, such as Search For Help On and How To Use Help, narrow down the Help topics.

When you choose a Help topic, the Help program is loaded into its own resizable, scrolling window, with menus from which you can choose commands. For example, you can use the menu commands to print the current Help topic, annotate a topic with your own comments, or insert a bookmark so that you can readily return to an important bit of information.

Choosing Annotate from Help's Edit menu displays a small text window in which you can add a note to the current Help topic for future reference. When you click Save to close the window, a small paper-clip icon appears next to the topic name. Just click the icon to display your note.

The Bookmark feature lets you add bookmarks to Help files so that you can move to often-referenced places quickly. To mark a section, choose Define from the Bookmark menu. Either accept the default bookmark name (the name of the current section), or type your own name. When you click OK, the name appears on the Bookmark menu. You can then choose the bookmark to move directly to that spot in the file.

Buttons at the top of the Help window take you to the contents for the current Help topic, allow you to search for a topic, go back to the last topic, see a list of the last several topics you needed help on, and display a glossary of common Help terms. When more than one screen of information is available, two buttons with arrows appear, allowing you to browse forward and backward through the Help file a page at a time.

A line appears under text when more information is available about a specific topic elsewhere in the Help file. When you point to the underlined text, the pointer changes to a hand icon, indicating that if you click the line, you will be taken directly to the additional information.

A dotted line appears under terms in a Help file when a pop-up definition is available for the term. Clicking the term displays the definition in a window. Click anywhere on the screen to close the pop-up window.

When you need advice

In the US, the telephone number for Microsoft Product Support Services is (206) 454-2030. A message may tell you to call an 800 number if you need sales and service. For questions about operating Windows, stay on the line and push the specified button to route your call to a Windows expert.

The About (*Program Name*) command, which is the last command on many Help menus, provides information about the active application in a window like this one:

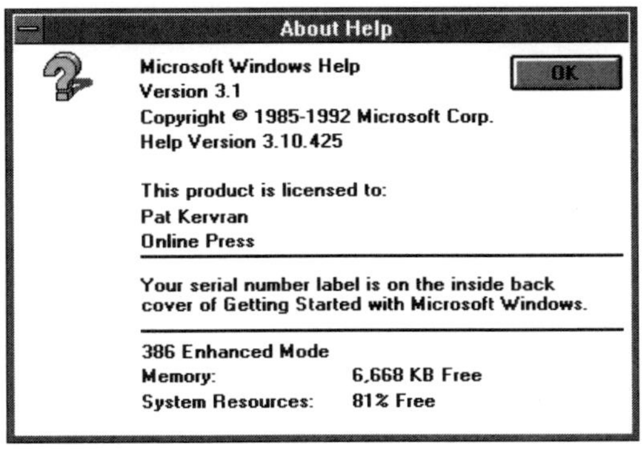

In addition to showing you the version number of the program, the About dialog box might tell you which mode Windows is running in, the percentage of system resources available, and how much free memory and disk space you have, as well as esoteric tidbits like whether or not your machine has a math coprocessor installed.

Context-Sensitive Help

In some Windows applications, you can use a keyboard shortcut to get to a Help topic quickly. For example, to get information about a command, highlight the command, and press F1. Windows displays the Help topic for that command. To get information about a dialog box, you can often press F1 or click the dialog box's Help button.

With this background information under your belt, you are ready to get started with the Windows program. If you have not yet installed Windows on your computer, turn to Appendix A. While using the Windows Setup program, you will have a chance to apply your knowledge about windows, dialog boxes, and a host of other features. If your computer is all set to start running Windows, head on to Chapter 2, where we get down to business with the program.

2

Windows Working Environment: Program Manager

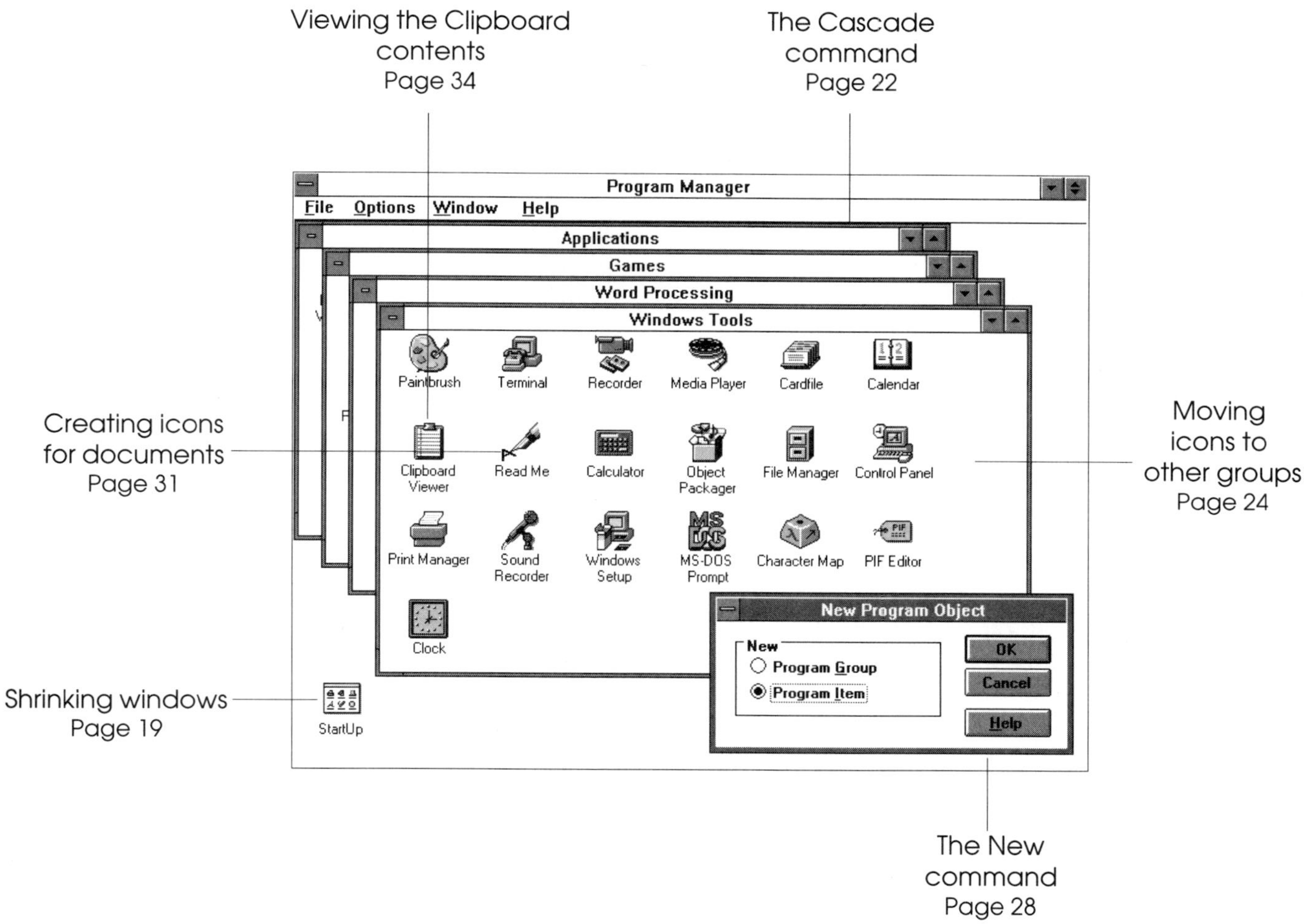

Viewing the Clipboard contents
Page 34
The Cascade command
Page 22
Creating icons for documents
Page 31
Moving icons to other groups
Page 24
Shrinking windows
Page 19
The New command
Page 28
Program Manager
File
Options
Window
Help
Applications
Games
Word Processing
Windows Tools
Paintbrush
Terminal
Recorder
Media Player
Cardfile
Calendar
Clipboard Viewer
Read Me
Calculator
Object Packager
File Manager
Control Panel
Print Manager
Sound Recorder
Windows Setup
MS-DOS Prompt
Character Map
PIF Editor
Clock
StartUp
New Program Object
New
Program Group
Program Item
OK
Cancel
Help

In Chapter 1 we explained some of the concepts behind Windows. Now you're ready to integrate this environment into your everyday work. Windows has two distinct components that help you get organized and thereby contribute to your productivity: Program Manager and File Manager. Program Manager helps you organize your work into logical, manageable groups and gives you the tools to create new files and manipulate existing ones. File Manager helps you clean up your hard disk so that your programs and documents are stored in an efficient, easily accessible manner. We cover File Manager in detail in Chapter 3. In this chapter, we introduce Program Manager.

When you first start Windows, Program Manager is loaded automatically, and it runs throughout your Windows session. If you have not already started Windows, follow these steps:

1. Type *win* at the C> prompt.
2. Press Enter.

That's all there is to it. The copyright screen makes a brief appearance, and then your computer displays the Program Manager window. Your screen looks something like this:

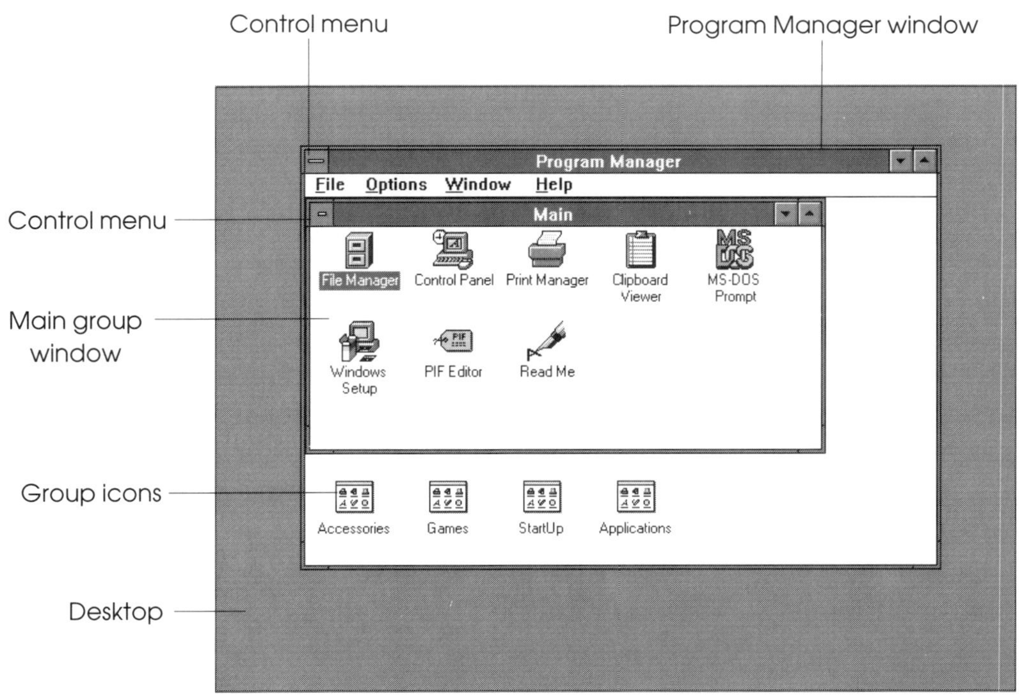

The neutral-color background that you see behind the Program Manager window is called the desktop. As we explained in Chapter 1, all your Windows programs and applications run in windows on the desktop, but because the windows sometimes fill the entire screen, the desktop is not always visible.

When you installed Windows on your computer, the Windows Setup program sorted the Windows component programs into groups, such as the Main group, the Accessories group, and the Games group. (Notice the icons at the bottom of the Program Manager window.) It also created a group called StartUp, which you can use to designate applications that you want to be automatically started each time you start Windows. If applications, such as Microsoft Word for Windows, were stored on your hard disk at the time of installation, Windows also created a group for them and assigned the group an icon.

Groups

The window that you now see in the middle of the screen displays the contents of the Main group, a collection of tools that come with Windows. The other groups have been "minimized" into icons at the bottom of the Program Manager window to reduce screen clutter. All groups appear either as windows or as icons within the Program Manager window.

Minimizing, Maximizing, and Restoring Windows

Windows allows you to minimize (shrink) windows into icons, maximize (expand) icons and windows to fill the entire screen, and restore icons and windows to their previous sizes. Try this:

Shrinking windows

1. Using the mouse, click the Minimize button, the downward-pointing arrow in the top-right corner of the Main window. The window shrinks into an icon and moves to the bottom of the Program Manager window, as shown on the next page.

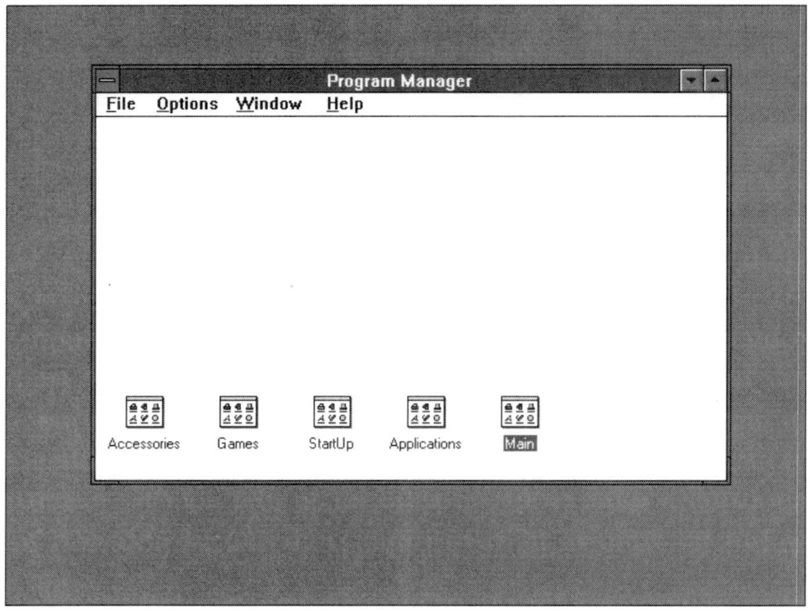

Notice that the name *Main* appears beneath the icon.

Expanding windows

2. Click the Maximize button (the upward-pointing arrow in the top-right corner of the Program Manager window) to fully expand the Program Manager window. The window expands to fill the screen, obscuring the desktop. Notice that the Maximize button is replaced by the Restore button (the double arrow) and that the window frame disappears, indicating that the window is fully maximized. (Because a maximized window doesn't have a frame, you can't manually resize it.)

Disappearing windows

Window "logic" can be baffling. Common problems are "lost" and obscured windows. Think of your open windows as playing cards in a deck. The topmost window is completely visible, but successive windows get buried. They are still there; they are just not visible. Press Alt+Esc repeatedly to bring open windows to the top of the stack.

Disappearing title bar

When you maximize a group window, the window's title bar seems to disappear. In reality, the title bar merges with the title bar and menu bar of the parent application. For example, if you maximize a group window in Program Manager, the Control menu and Restore button move to Program Manager's menu bar. The title of the group moves to Program Manager's title bar, to read something like Program Manager - [Windows Tools]. Most Windows applications follow this convention, and maximizing a document window will have a similar effect.

3. Click the Restore button. The Program Manager window reverts to its original size. (You can also restore a window by double-clicking its title bar.)

Restoring windows to their previous size

Now take a few moments to experiment with manually resizing the window:

1. Move the pointer to any side or corner of the Program Manager window frame, and when the pointer changes to a double-headed arrow, click the frame and drag it in either of the directions indicated by the arrows.

Manually resizing windows

2. Click the Maximize button to expand the window again.
3. To redisplay the Main window, simply double-click the Main icon at the bottom of the Program Manager window.

Arranging Windows

After opening several windows, you might find that your screen is a jumble of obscured and partially visible windows. You can manually arrange the windows by dragging their title bars, but two commands on the Window menu, Tile and Cascade, automate this task. Let's experiment:

1. Open the Accessories window by double-clicking its icon at the bottom of the screen. The Accessories window opens and partially obscures the Main window.

Wrong window minimized?

If you minimize a window by mistake, you can easily restore the window to its original size by double-clicking its icon. Then minimize the correct window.

Unshrinkable menu bars

Although you can make an application window very small, Windows won't let you shrink the application window so much that the menu bar doesn't fit. As you start shrinking the window, the menu names wrap on the menu bar until they are stacked on top of one another in a very tall (and difficult to use) menu bar.

The versatile title bar

In addition to displaying the window's name and indicating whether the window is active or not, the title bar provides a few other services. You can drag the title bar to manually reposition the window, and you can also double-click the title bar to maximize or restore the window.

Moving windows

2. Experiment with moving the windows by dragging their title bars. When you click any part of a partially obscured window, it is displayed on top of the "stack" of windows, and its title bar changes to a darker color, indicating that the window is active. (The active window will be affected by any commands you choose.)

Moving windows manually will often get the job done, but you can move only one window at a time. And if a window is totally obscured, you can't click it to move it. Here's how to automatically arrange all open windows:

The Cascade command

1. Choose Cascade from the Window menu. As shown here, the two open windows arrange themselves in a neat stack:

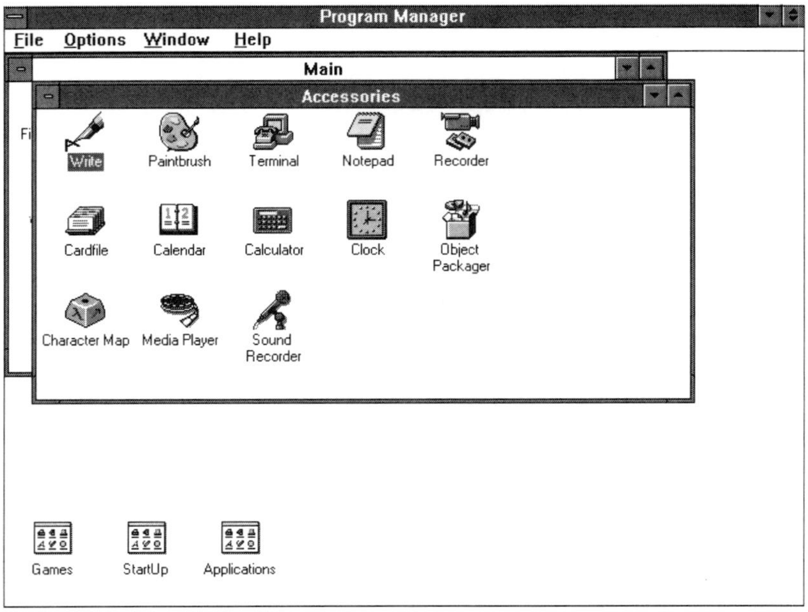

As you can see, only the title bar and the left edge of the obscured bottom window is now showing. Notice that the title bar of the top window is dark in color, indicating that it is the active window.

Activating windows

You have seen that clicking a window's title bar makes the window active. You can also activate a group's window by choosing the group name from the Window menu, which lists all the groups available in Program Manager, whether or not their windows are open. Choosing a group that has been minimized to an icon opens the group's window.

Although the Cascade command neatly arranges the windows, you might prefer to position them so that you can see as much of each window as possible. For this purpose, you use the Tile command, which arranges all open windows within the Program Manager window like tiles on a kitchen counter. Try this:

The Tile command

1. Choose Tile from the Window menu. The windows reposition themselves so that they each take up about half of the screen, with space left at the bottom for the other group icons, as shown here:

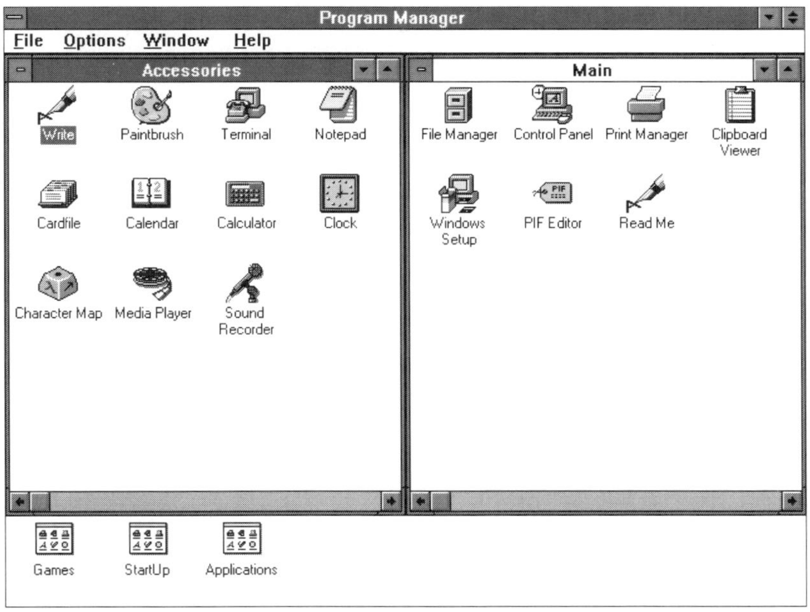

Although Tile may seem like the obvious choice to organize your workspace, it can create confusion when you have several windows open at once. After you use the Tile command, group windows that contain many icons might not have room to display them all. Use the Cascade command if you are arranging more than four or five windows.

Reorganizing Groups

One of the great things about Windows is that it is highly customizable. In Program Manager, you can reorganize, delete, copy, and even create program groups and icons to suit your needs. For example, when you start working with Windows, you might find yourself wondering why Windows organized its component programs the way it did. In particular, you might find that the separation of certain programs into Main and Accessories groups is confusing and even illogical. Putting them all into one group is as easy as dragging their icons from one window to another. (You can have as many as 50 icons in a group.) Try the following:

1. Activate the Main window by clicking anywhere within it.
2. If necessary, scroll until you can see the File Manager icon (the filing cabinet), and then click the icon to make it active. The name under the icon is highlighted.

Moving icons to other groups

3. Hold down the mouse button, and drag the icon into the Accessories window. As you drag the icon, the name under the icon disappears, and its colors might change.
4. Release the mouse button. Here's the result:

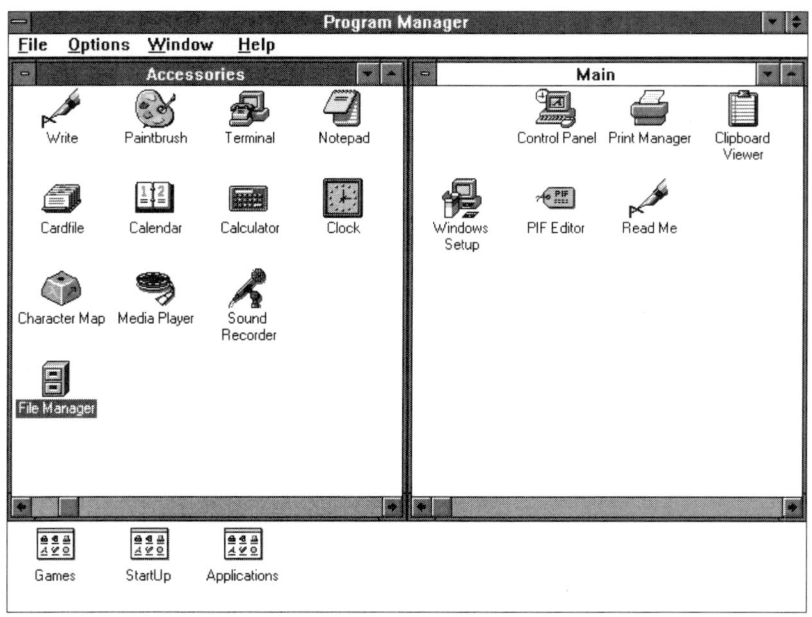

5. Repeat steps 1 through 4 for all the other icons in the Main window. (If necessary, scroll the window to find them all.)

Now all the icons for the programs that came with Windows (except for the games) are in one group. Don't worry about arranging the icons neatly in the Accessories window for now—you will rearrange them later.

Directories vs. groups

Organizing your programs into groups in Program Manager does not affect the way your directories and files are stored. You use groups to visually arrange program icons for ease of use under Program Manager. However, moving a program icon from one group to another does not actually move the program on your hard disk.

Deleting Obsolete Groups

If reorganizing the programs and documents in your groups results in a group that no longer contains any icons, you can delete the group so that it does not get in your way. (If it turns out later that you need the group, you can always re-create it, as discussed on page 27.)

Now that the Main group is empty, follow these steps to delete it:

1. Check to be sure that the Main window is active (its title bar is dark in color).
2. Choose Delete from the File menu. Windows displays this warning message:

The Delete command

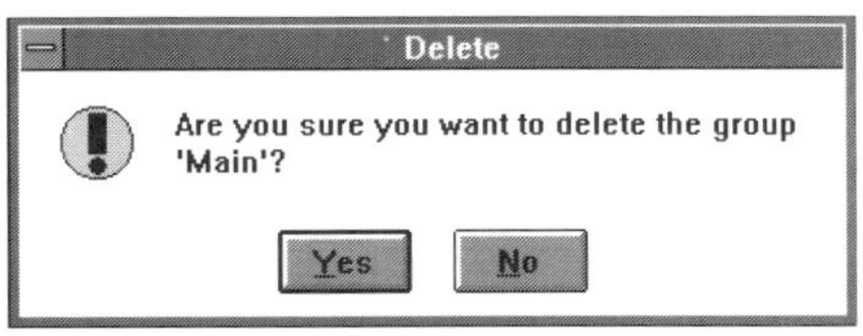

3. Click Yes. The Main window disappears from the screen, and the Accessories window becomes active.

Arranging Icons

Messy windows are hard to work with, and the more icons you add to a group, the messier the group's window can

No lone-wolf icons

Icons must be placed in a group. You can place them in groups by dragging them to group windows or by dragging them to minimized group window icons, but they must be part of a group. If you try to place an icon outside a group window, the icon turns into a circle with a diagonal slash through it, indicating that you can't do it.

No groups within groups

Group windows cannot be placed within other group windows. Group windows are strictly one-dimensional and are intended only to organize icons into logical collections. If you try to move a minimized window into another group window, the group icon simply floats above the window, and you cannot activate it.

Jumping to icons

If you add many icons to a window, you might have a hard time finding your program's icon. A quick way to jump to an icon is to activate the window, and type the first letter of the program's name. This selects the icon, and scrolls the window to bring the icon into view. If you have more than one program with the same first letter, press the letter repeatedly to cycle among all the programs whose names start with that letter.

become. You'll probably want to straighten up the icons in the Accessories window to make them easier to locate. You could do this by carefully positioning each icon with the mouse, but there is an easier way:

The Arrange Icons command

1. With the Accessories window active, choose Arrange Icons from the Window menu. Windows aligns the icons so that they fit in the Accessories window in perfect rows and columns, something like this:

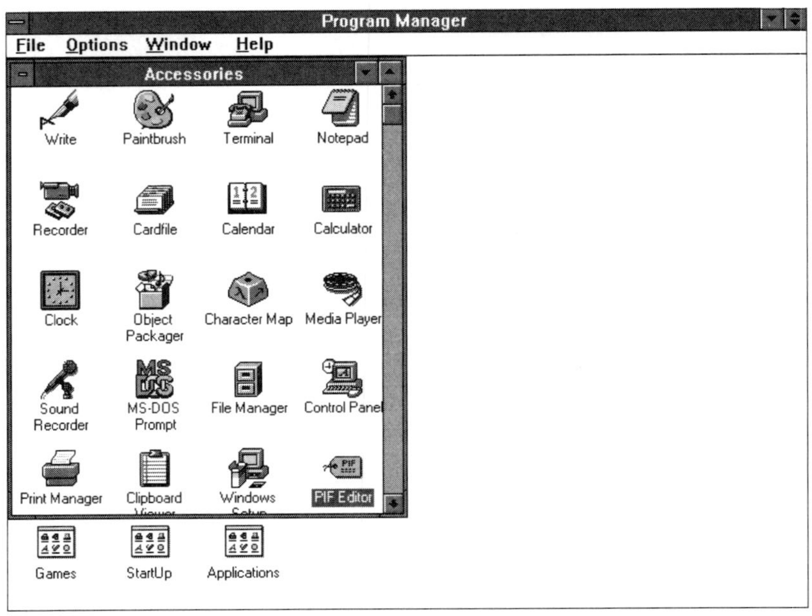

Scroll bars appear on the right and bottom sides of the window if the icons don't all fit in the window.

Windows can also automatically rearrange icons for you each time you open a window, change its size, add items, or move items. To turn on this feature:

The Auto Arrange command

1. Pull down the Options menu. If you don't see a check mark in front of the Auto Arrange command, choose Auto Arrange to make it active.

Renaming Groups

The current name of the Accessories group no longer fits the collection of programs in the group, so let's change the name to something more appropriate. Here's how:

1. Shrink the Accessories window to an icon by clicking the Minimize button in the top-right corner of the window.
2. Make the Accessories icon active by clicking it once. A menu pops up above the icon. This is the icon's Control menu, and you can ignore it for now. (We discussed the Control menu on page 6.)
3. Choose the Properties command from the File menu. Windows displays this dialog box, with the group name highlighted:

The Properties command

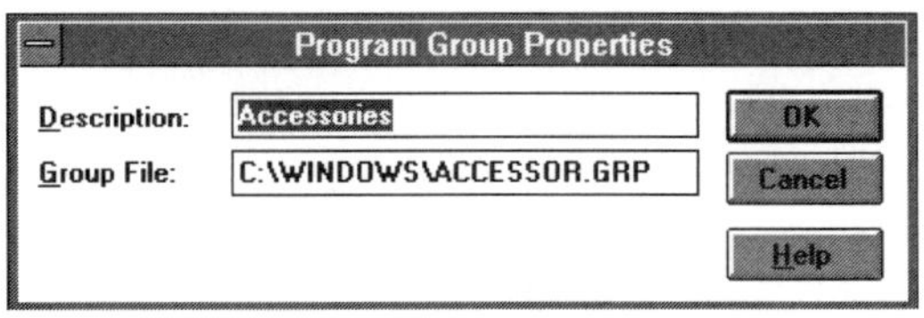

4. Type *Windows Tools* as the new name for the group, and then click OK. The new name replaces the old one beneath the group icon at the bottom of the Program Manager window. Note that the characters of the new name appear with the uppercase and lowercase letters you typed in the Description text box.
5. Double-click the Windows Tools icon to expand it into a window. The new name for the group appears in the window's title bar.

You can change the name of any group icon to a name of up to 30 characters. You can also change the name of any program or document icon to a name of up to 40 characters. Changing the name of a Windows icon doesn't change the name of the actual document or application it represents. As far as DOS is concerned, the document or application still has its original name of eight or fewer characters. The icon name is merely a device that enables you to more easily manage files within Windows.

Activating the next window

A quick way to activate windows or group window icons in Program Manager is to use the Next command, which is on the Control menu of all group windows. Choosing this command activates the window or window icon that was opened after the currently active window. You can also press Ctrl+Tab to cycle quickly through windows.

Creating New Groups

You now know enough to organize other groups in Program Manager to suit your needs. One constructive technique is to create a group for each of your current projects and to include in the group all relevant applications and documents. Then double-clicking a project group icon automatically opens a window that puts everything you need to work on that project at your fingertips.

To demonstrate the process, let's create a new group to hold word-processing applications, including the Notepad and Write programs that come with Windows and any other writing programs you might have, such as Word for Windows. We'll also create two simple documents and store them as document icons with the writing programs. Using the same techniques, you could create a group called *Correspondence* in which to keep business letters, or a group called *Quarterly Projections* for spreadsheets. Follow these steps:

The New command

1. Choose the New command from the File menu. Windows displays this dialog box:

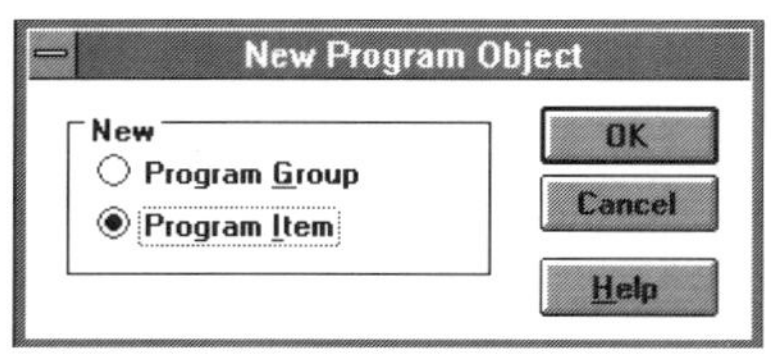

2. Click the Program Group button, and then click OK. The New Program Object dialog box is replaced by this Program Group Properties dialog box:

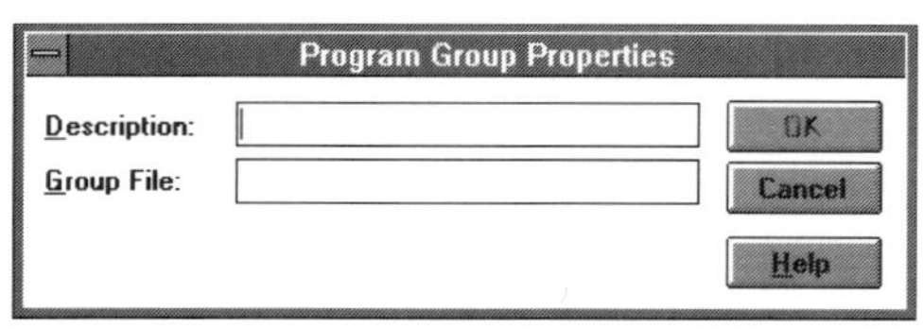

3. In the Description text box, type *Word Processing*, the name for the new group, and click OK. A new, empty group window appears, overlapping the Windows Tools window.
4. Choose the Tile command from the Window menu. The windows reposition themselves on the screen like this:

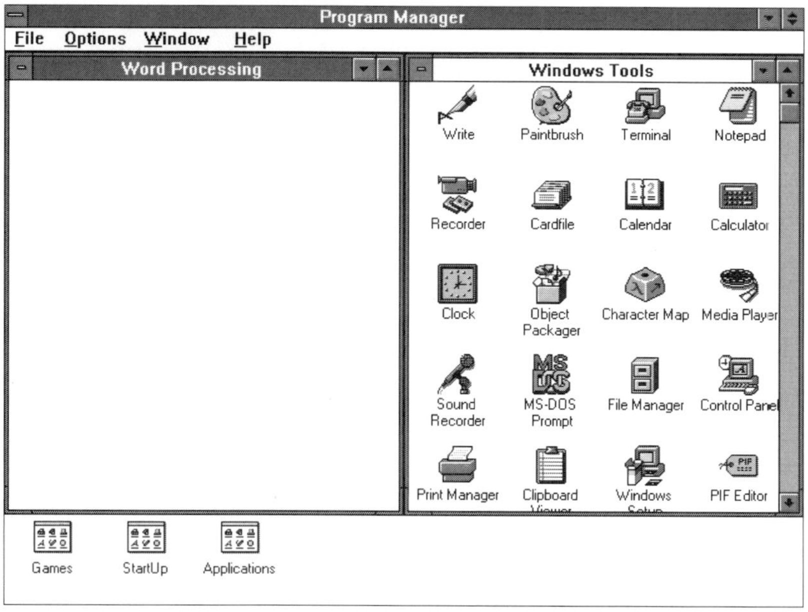

5. If necessary, scroll the Windows Tools window until you can see the Write icon—a pen writing the letter *A*.
6. Click the Write icon, drag the icon into the Word Processing window, and release the mouse button.
7. Click the Notepad icon, drag the icon into the Word Processing window, and release the mouse button.

You can repeat this procedure for any other Windows word processors you own, such as Word for Windows or Ami Pro. (Their icons were placed either in the Applications group by the Windows Setup program, or in another group window by their own installation programs.) You can also use the new Word Processing group to store icons for non-Windows applications, such as Word or WordPerfect.

Creating Documents

Next, we'll create a simple document in the Word Processing group and watch Windows assign it an appropriate icon. For this purpose, you'll use Notepad, the handy text editor that is shipped with Windows. Notepad is useful for jotting down notes or creating and editing short text documents.

For demonstration purposes, assume that CityRock Gym—a sports club in Emeryville, California, that features indoor rock climbing and weight training—is investigating the cost of purchasing a small public-address system. During a phone conversation, Peter Mayfield, the club's manager, uses Notepad to take down information about a potential supplier. Let's follow along:

Starting Notepad

1. Double-click the Notepad icon in the Word Processing window. The Notepad application opens with a blank, untitled document displayed. Notice that the Notepad window is not maximized, allowing you to see parts of other windows. In Chapter 4, you'll learn how to activate these windows so that you can switch among open applications and move information from one to another.
2. The blinking insertion point in the top-left corner of the Notepad window indicates that you can begin typing, so type *Allphone, Inc.* (the supplier's name), and press Enter.
3. Type *4107 Lake Louis Ave, Ste 44*, and press Enter.
4. Type *Emeryville, CA 94608*, and press Enter.
5. Type *(415) 666-2000*, and press Enter. Your screen now looks like this:

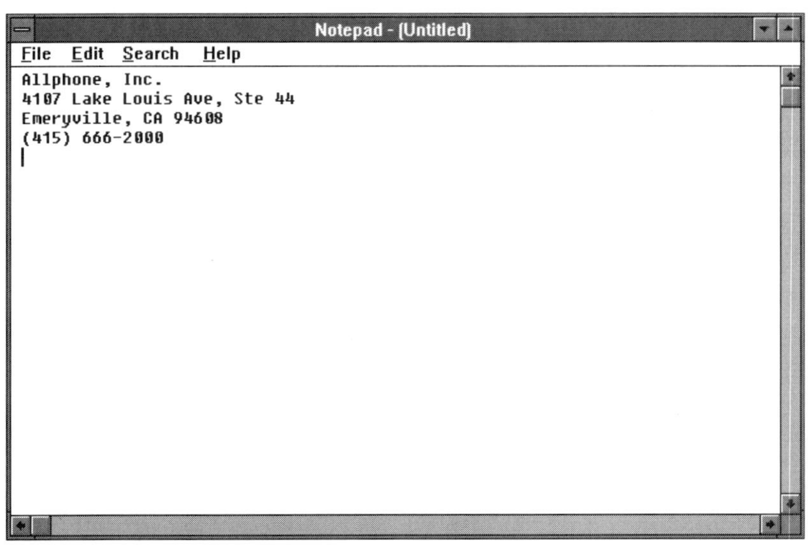

Now let's save the document:

The Save As command

1. Choose the Save As command from Notepad's File menu to display this dialog box:

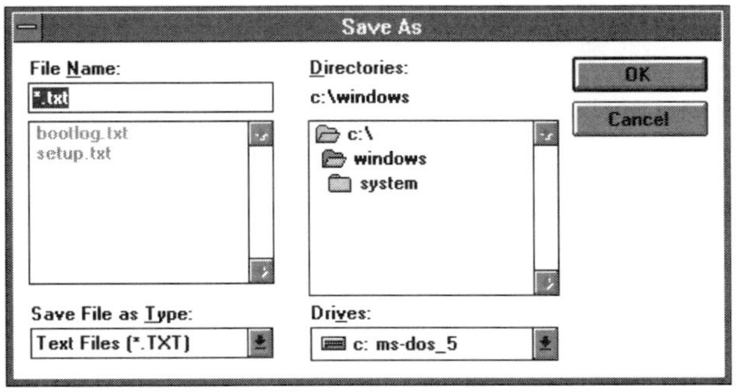

2. In the File Name text box, type *pubsys* (for *public-address system*), and click OK. Because you haven't specified a directory and filename extension, the document is saved in the WINDOWS directory and is given the extension TXT, which indicates that the file was created by the Notepad program. When the file is saved, the name of the file, PUBSYS.TXT, appears in the title bar of the window.

The Exit command

3. Choose the Exit command from the File menu. The Notepad window closes, and you return to Program Manager.

Creating icons for documents

Next, you need to create an icon to represent the document in the Word Processing window. You can give the icon any

Control menu commands

Every window has a Control menu represented by the minus sign in the box in the window's top-left corner. To choose a Control menu command, click the box to display the menu, and then click the command you want. From the keyboard, press Alt+Hyphen (-) to access the Control menu.

Window closing shortcut

To quickly close a window, simply double-click the Control menu box in the window's top-left corner. If the window doesn't close, try double-clicking even faster.

Exiting gracefully

The Exit command can be found on the File menu of almost all Windows applications. It allows you to quit the current application and return to the previously opened program. If an application doesn't have a File menu, use the Close command on the application's Control menu to close the window.

name that will help you remember what the document is about, as long as the name has fewer than 40 characters. Follow these steps:

1. Be sure the Word Processing window is active. (If it isn't, click it.) Then choose New from the File menu to display the New Program Object dialog box.

2. Check that Program Item is selected, and click OK. This Program Item Properties dialog box appears:

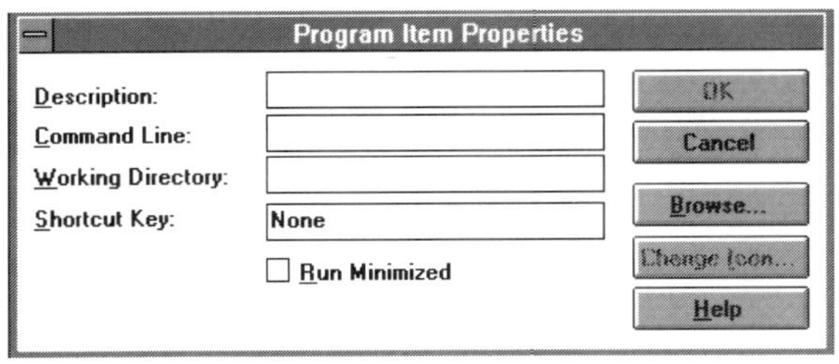

3. In the Description text box, type *PA System* as the name of this document.

4. Click the Command Line text box, and link the new icon with the Notepad document by typing *c:\windows\pubsys.txt.* (This "path" gives Windows the "address" of the document. In effect, you are telling Windows that it can find the document called PUBSYS.TXT in the WINDOWS directory on drive C.) If you can't remember the exact path or name of the file, you can click the Browse button to display a dialog box that you can use to locate the file.

5. Click OK to close the Program Item Properties dialog box and return to Program Manager. As shown on the next page, the new Notepad icon with the name *PA System* below it appears in the Word Processing window. As you can see, Windows has automatically assigned a Notepad icon to the document as a helpful reminder of the application in which it was created. In Windows terminology, the document is now *associated* with the application.

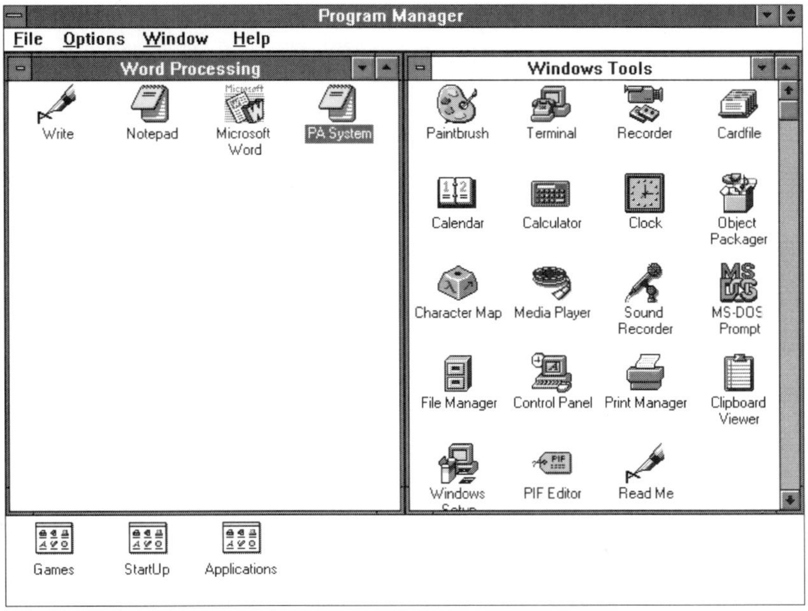

Transferring Information via the Clipboard

Imagine that later in the day, Peter Mayfield decides to transfer the supplier's name and address from the Notepad document to a Write document so that he can write a letter inquiring about the supplier's public-address systems. Here are the steps:

1. Double-click the PA System icon in the Word Processing group window. The Notepad program automatically starts with the PUBSYS.TXT document open in a Notepad window.

Selecting text

2. Select the text in the window by pointing to the left of the first character of the supplier's name, holding down the left mouse button, dragging down and to the right until all the information is highlighted, and releasing the mouse button.

The Copy command

3. Choose Copy from the Edit menu to copy the selection to the Clipboard.
4. Choose Exit from the File menu.

Although you have closed the Notepad window, the copied text still exists on the Clipboard, a temporary storage place in memory for cut or copied data. The information stays on the Clipboard until it is replaced by the next item you cut or copy, or until you exit Windows. If you shut down your computer in the middle of a work session or the power goes off, this information is lost. Let's sidetrack here for a moment to make sure the text is on the Clipboard:

Viewing the Clipboard contents

1. Double-click the Clipboard Viewer icon in the Windows Tools window. This Clipboard Viewer window opens, revealing the text you have copied.

2. Close the Clipboard Viewer by choosing the Exit command from the File menu or by double-clicking the Control menu box in the top-left corner of the window.

The next step is to paste the copied text into a Write document:

Clipboard Viewer

The Clipboard is an area of memory for temporary storage of cut or copied data. Clipboard Viewer is a Windows tool that allows you to view that data. You cannot manipulate the data, even though Clipboard Viewer has an Edit menu. The only actions you can take, besides simple viewing, are to save the Clipboard contents as a file or to clear the contents.

Saving the Clipboard contents

You can save the contents of the Clipboard as a file for later use. Open the Clipboard Viewer window, and choose Save As from the File menu. Enter a filename, and click OK. Clipboard Viewer saves the file with a CLP extension so that it can recognize and open the file later. Opening a CLP file replaces the current contents of the Clipboard.

Freeing memory

If you are running low on memory, clearing the Clipboard contents might free up some space. Double-click Clipboard Viewer's icon to open its window, and if you are sure you don't need the Clipboard contents, choose Delete from the Edit menu. Click Yes when asked to confirm this action.

1. Double-click the Write icon in the Word Processing window. Windows starts the Write program, which then displays a blank document window.

Starting Write

2. Choose Paste from the Edit menu. The text you copied from the Notepad document now appears in the Write window.

The Paste command

3. Complete the letter of inquiry with the date, a brief description of the system you need, and a request for information.
4. Now save the document by choosing Save As from the File menu. The Save As dialog box appears so that you can give the Write document a name.
5. Type *pas50592* (for *public-address system inquiry on May 5, 1992*), and then click OK. The name of the document, PAS50592.WRI, appears in the Write window's title bar. (Write gives all its documents the extension WRI unless you tell it otherwise.)
6. Close the window and quit the Write program by choosing Exit from the File menu or by double-clicking the Control menu box.

Assigning Icons and Shortcut Keys

To create an icon for the letter, you could repeat the steps you went through to assign an icon to the PUBSYS.TXT document, but here we'll take the opportunity to show you another way. This method involves copying the Write icon, then changing its properties so that the application starts and opens the document either when you double-click the icon or when you press a shortcut key combination. Try this:

1. While holding down the Ctrl key, click the Write icon, and drag it to another place within the Word Processing window to create a copy of the icon.

Copying an icon

2. With the second Write icon active, hold down the Alt key and double-click the icon to display the Program Item Properties dialog box. (This is an alternative way of choosing Properties from the File menu.)

Properties shortcut

3. In the Description text box, type *PA System Letter*.

4. Double-click the Command Line text box to highlight the WRITE.EXE entry, and type *pas50592.wri*. Notice that you didn't type the document's entire path this time because, by default, Write saves its documents in the WINDOWS directory. If the document was located elsewhere, you would need to type the document's full path.

5. Click anywhere in the Shortcut Key text box, and type the letter *p*. (You can use any single letter, number, or function key except F1.) The word *None* in the text box is replaced by Ctrl+Alt+P.

6. Click OK.

When you return to Program Manager, the Word Processing window looks like this:

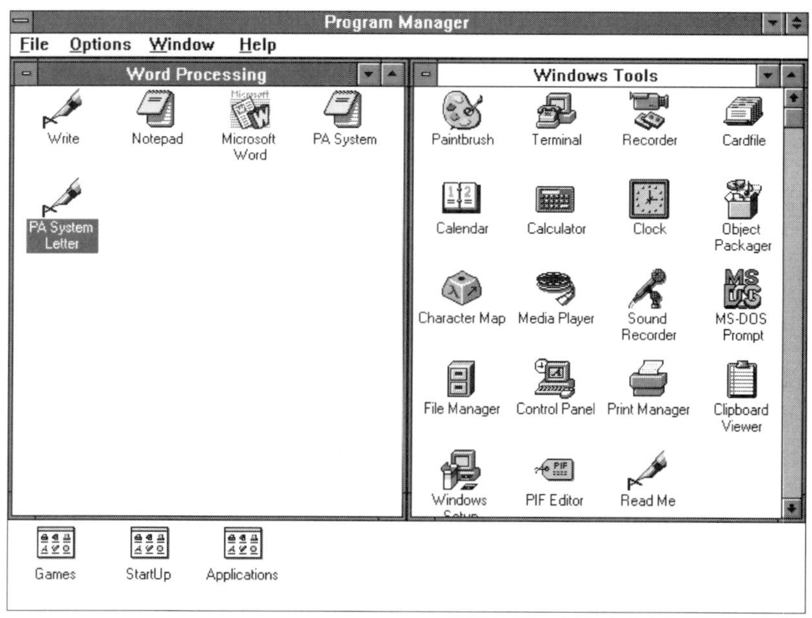

Notice that the name of the second Write icon is now PA System Letter. Double-clicking this icon starts the Write program and opens the PAS50592.WRI document. As long as Program Manager is active, pressing the key combination you assigned to the icon—in this case, Ctrl+Alt+P—does the same thing.

Let's try both ways:

1. Double-click the PA System Letter icon in the Word Processing window. The PAS50592.WRI document opens in a Write window.
2. Choose Exit from the Write program's File menu, or double-click the Control menu box.
3. Open the document again by pressing Ctrl+Alt+P (the shortcut key combination).

   Using the shortcut key
4. Choose Exit again to leave Write.

Creating Icons for New Applications

You can run Windows Setup—the Windows installation program—to have Windows create Program Manager icons for any new applications you acquire. However, Setup recognizes some programs and ignores others. If you want to create an icon for a new application, here is a quick, surefire way to do it:

1. Activate the window of the group to which you want to add the application (for example, the Word Processing window), and choose New from the File menu.
2. In the New Program Object dialog box, be sure the Program Item option is selected, and then click OK to display the Program Item Properties dialog box.

The Run command

To start either a Windows or non-Windows program that you use infrequently and for which you don't want to create an icon, choose the Run command from Program Manager's File menu, type the program's name in the Command Line text box, and click OK. If the program you want is not located in the current directory, type the entire path (see page 32).

The StartUp group

When Setup created your groups, it also created a group called StartUp. If you use an application each time you use Windows and you want it to start automatically, put a copy of its icon in the StartUp group. The next time you start Windows, the application will start after Program Manager.

3. Type a name for the application in the Description text box, and type the application's path (see page 32 for more information about paths) in the Command Line text box.

4. So that you can select an icon for the application, click the Change Icon button. If a *Change Icon* warning message appears, simply click OK. Windows displays a Change Icon dialog box similar to this one:

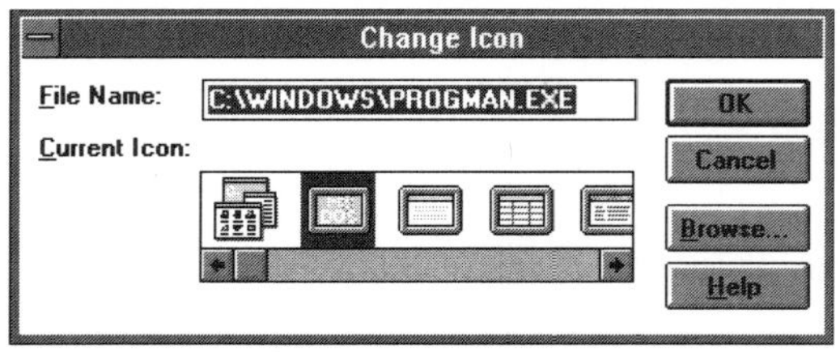

5. Use the scroll bar to look through the available icons, select one by clicking it, and click OK to close the Change Icon dialog box. The icon you selected now appears in the Program Item Properties dialog box.

6. Click OK to close the dialog box and return to Program Manager.

   The application's new icon is displayed in the active group. Double-clicking this icon will now start the application.

Cleaning Up and Exiting

If you have followed along with our examples, your Program Manager window might be a bit of a mess, with various icons and windows strewn about. Now is a good time to get organized before moving on to the next chapter.

1. Open all the remaining group windows by double-clicking the group icons at the bottom of the screen. You probably have at least one group that you haven't yet inspected. (Take a look at the Games group, which includes the Windows games Solitaire and Minesweeper.)

2. Choose Cascade from the Window menu. Your windows reposition themselves in a neat stack.

After you've positioned your windows to your liking, you will want to save the arrangement. The only way to do this is to quit Windows. Let's do that now:

Saving your window and icon arrangement

1. First, be sure that the Save Settings On Exit command on the Options menu has a check mark beside it. This setting saves the arrangement of your group windows and icons for your next Windows session.

The Exit Windows command

2. Choose Exit Windows from the Program Manager File menu. This Exit Windows dialog box appears, warning you that you are about to end your Windows session:

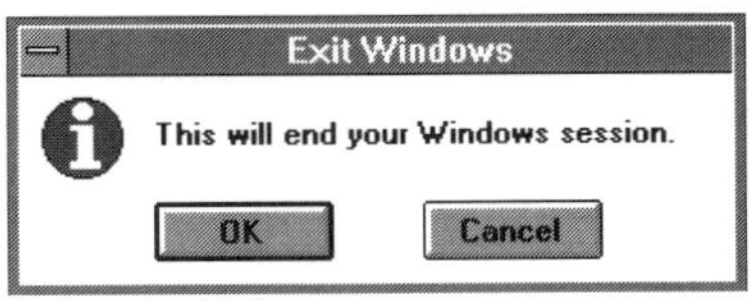

3. Click OK to save your window and icon arrangement and exit Windows.

That's all there is to it. We covered a lot of information in this chapter, and you might be feeling a bit overwhelmed. However, after you perform these tasks once or twice, they'll seem like old hat.

3 Organizing Your Files: File Manager

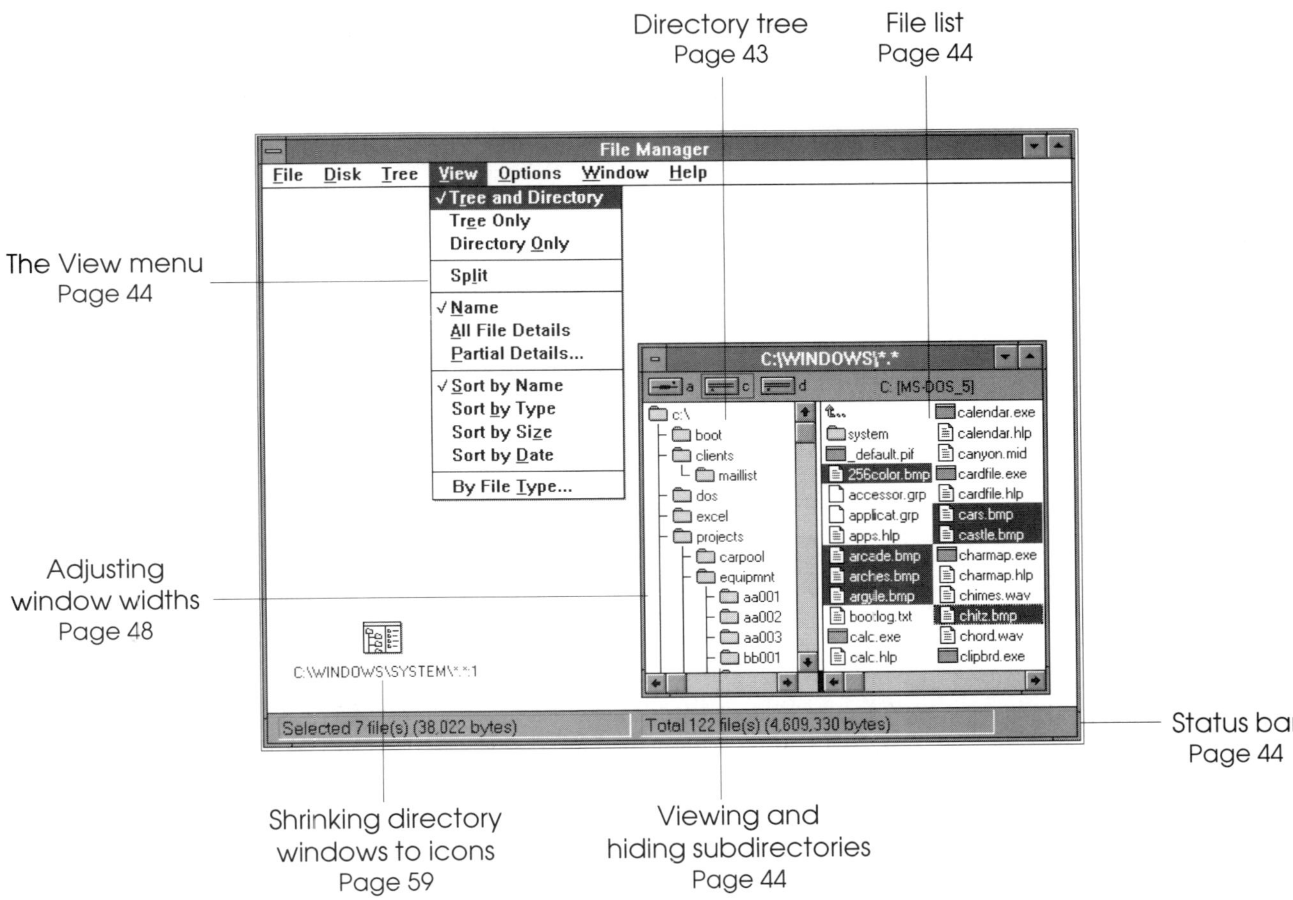

Directory tree
Page 43
File list
Page 44
The View menu
Page 44
Adjusting
window widths
Page 48
Status bar
Page 44
Shrinking directory
windows to icons
Page 59
Viewing and
hiding subdirectories
Page 44
File Manager
File Disk Tree View Options Window Help
✓Tree and Directory
Tree Only
Directory Only
Split
✓Name
All File Details
Partial Details...
✓Sort by Name
Sort by Type
Sort by Size
Sort by Date
By File Type...
C:\WINDOWS*.*
C: [MS-DOS_5]
Selected 7 file(s) (38,022 bytes)
Total 122 file(s) (4,609,330 bytes)

For some people, keeping computer files organized has always been a difficult chore. They'll load a program, start a new document, save it with a name such as JOHN.LET or EXPENSES.DAT, and think they'll be able to retrieve the document without much trouble if they ever need it again. Because these people are busy, they often don't take the time to work out a directory- and file-naming system, and they may end up searching directory after directory for the particular file they need. Is it JOHN.LET? Or JSMITH.LET? Or JS1-14.LET? And is it stored in the CORRESP directory, the PROJECTS directory, or the ACCT-REC directory?

With Windows, you no longer have to trust your memory to organize and retrieve documents efficiently. The Windows File Manager program is a powerful hard-disk organizational aid that displays the available directories as "tree" diagrams and offers a wide selection of file-management tools.

Starting File Manager

To start File Manager, simply double-click the File Manager icon—the one that looks like a file cabinet—in Program Manager. (If you followed along with the examples in the last chapter, the icon is in the Windows Tools group. Otherwise, the icon is in the Main group.) When you start File Manager, its window looks something like the one shown at the top of the facing page.

File Manager icons

Your File Manager window reflects the way your hard disk is set up and whether you are working on a network. As with Program Manager, everything you see in File Manager appears in a window or as an icon. By default, clicking the File Manager icon opens not only the File Manager window but also a window labeled with the path to the WINDOWS directory window. Below the title bar of this window are icons representing your floppy-disk drives, your hard drives (or hard-drive partitions), and, if you are connected to a network, the available network drives. A letter to the right of each drive icon identifies the drive, and network drive icons are further identified by the letters *NET*.

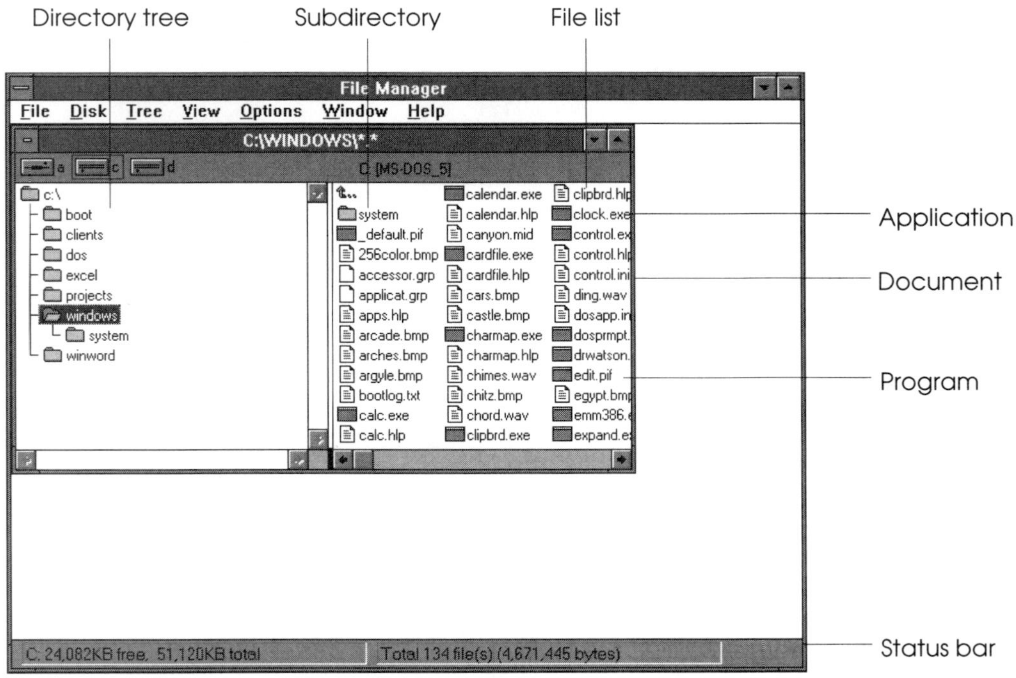

Directory tree

When you start File Manager, the directory window contains, at a minimum, icons for a floppy drive (A) and a single hard drive (C). File Manager highlights the C drive icon and displays in the left side of the window a visual diagram, called a directory tree, of the drive's structure. The directories that "branch" from the main, or root, directory on your C drive are represented by folder icons. The display includes, at a

Starting Windows at the File Manager window

You can have File Manager (or any other program) automatically start right after Program Manager whenever you start Windows. Use Notepad to open the WIN.INI file, which is stored in the WINDOWS directory. The file's fourth line should be RUN=. Click an insertion point after the equal sign, and type *winfile.exe* (the name of File Manager's program file). Then use the Save command to save the WIN.INI file. The next time you start Windows, Program Manager minimizes to an icon and File Manager opens, allowing you to use File Manager as your base of operations. You can switch back to Program Manager at any time simply by pressing Alt+Esc. (We discuss toggling between windows in Chapter 4.)

minimum, folder icons for a DOS directory (which stores operating-system files) and a WINDOWS directory. File Manager highlights the current directory, WINDOWS, and displays a list of all the files and subdirectories in that directory in the right side of the window. Executable files (those with PIF, EXE, BAT, and COM extensions) have rectangular icons with a thin bar across the top; and document files (those created with a specific program) have rectangular icons with thin rules across them, resembling a sheet of paper with one corner turned down.

File list

Status bar

In the status bar at the bottom of the File Manager window, a message tells you how much free space and how much total space you have on the current drive, how many files are in the current directory, and how much space they occupy.

Displaying Directories

You can expand and contract directories, displaying only the highest directory levels or zooming in for a closer look at subdirectories and files. Let's take a moment to experiment with hiding and displaying directories.

1. First, be sure that your display is set up as follows so that your screen will match our graphics:

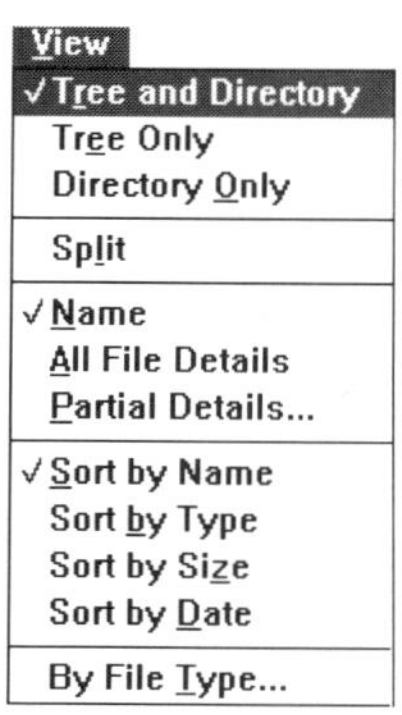

- On the View menu, the Tree And Directory, Name, and Sort By Name commands should be chosen (have check marks in front of them). If they aren't, choose them now.
- Also on the View menu, choose By File Type. In the By File Type dialog box, check that *.* appears in the Name text box and that all the check boxes in the File Type section have been selected.
- Finally, choose Indicate Expandable Branches from the Tree menu.

Viewing and hiding subdirectories

When Indicate Expandable Branches is turned on, some folder icons have a plus symbol to indicate that subdirectories "branch" from the directory represented by that icon. You can view the subdirectories by double-clicking the icon. A minus symbol on a folder icon indicates that you can hide its subdirectories.

2. Double-click the C:\ folder. The folder icons representing subdirectories disappear (collapse), and the minus symbol on the C:\ folder icon becomes a plus symbol. The files and directories in the root directory are now displayed in the file list on the right side of the window, as shown here:

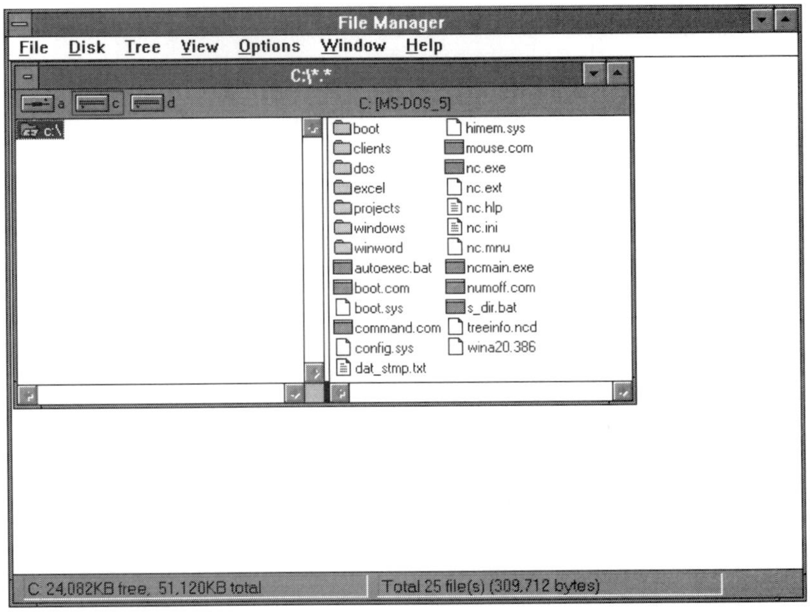

3. Double-click the C:\ folder icon again. The folder icons reappear (expand), and the plus symbol reverts to a minus symbol.

4. Double-click the WINDOWS folder icon to display its contents in the right side of the window, as shown on the next page.

Wildcards

The asterisk (*) and the question mark (?) are "wildcard" characters that allow you to select specific files. An * matches anything that follows it. A ? matches any single character. For example, *.* matches all filenames and all extensions, *.INV matches all files with an INV extension, and CHAP?.DOC matches all files with the DOC extension whose names start with CHAP followed by any single character.

The View menu

The View menu commands allow you to customize what appears in the File Manager window. You can choose to display just the directory tree, just the file list, or both. You can view files based on name, date, size, or file type. Choose the By File Type and Partial Details commands to fine-tune the display even further.

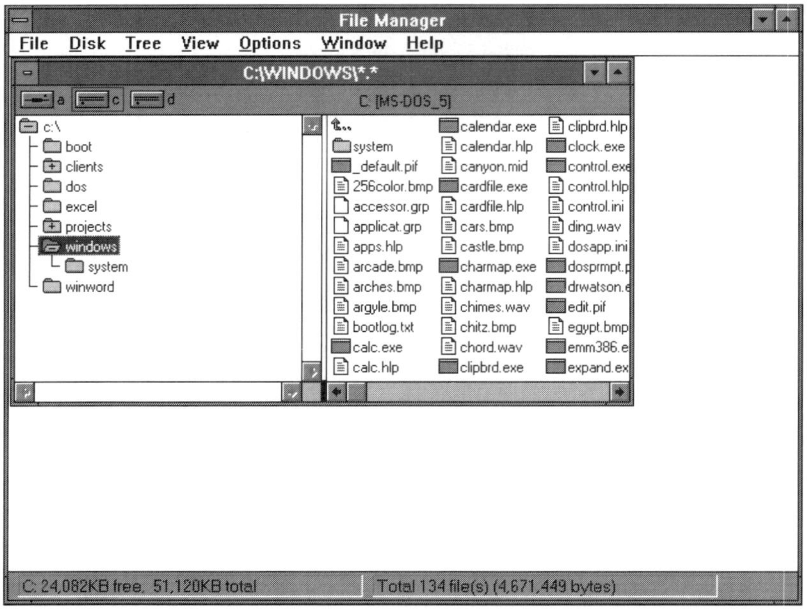

The WINDOWS directory has, at a minimum, a SYSTEM subdirectory. Some Windows applications automatically create their own subdirectories in the WINDOWS directory. Notice in the right side of the window that folder icons representing subdirectories appear with the files stored in the WINDOWS directory.

Instead of double-clicking folders one by one to display their contents, you can tell File Manager to display all subdirectories, like this:

Saving settings

After you've adjusted File Manager to display directories and files the way you want them, you'll want to save your settings. Be sure the Save Settings On Exit command on the Options menu is selected (has a check mark before it). Then when you exit File Manager, your settings are automatically saved.

The SYSTEM directory

The SYSTEM directory contains the files necessary to run Windows. A complex environment like Windows is the sum of many parts. The SYSTEM directory houses programs used to print, draw the screen, display fonts, recognize mouse actions, produce sounds, and interpret keyboard input, as well as carry out other behind-the-scenes functions.

Displaying all subdirectories

1. Choose Expand All from the Tree menu. File Manager opens all the folder icons in the directory tree, as shown here:

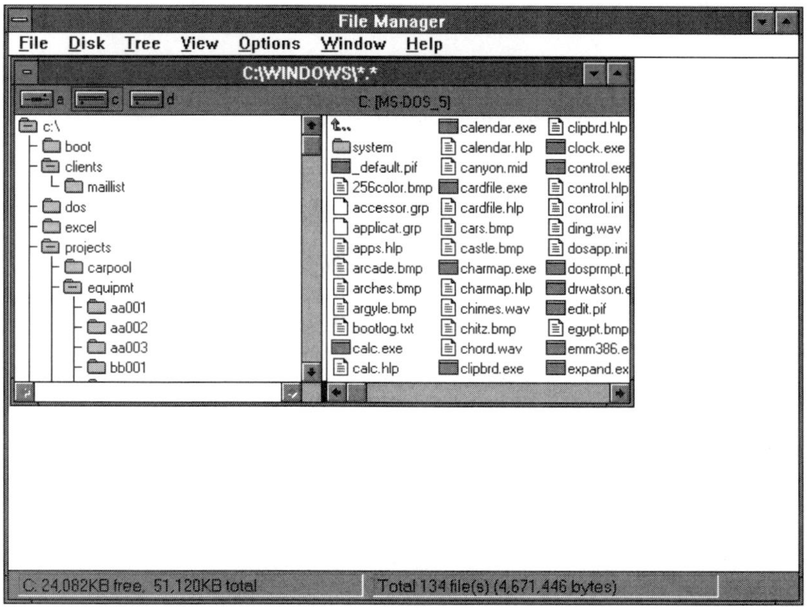

Enlarging the directory tree

If your WINDOWS directory has more subdirectories than will fit in the window, you can use the scroll bars below and to the right of the directory tree to scroll around. You can also drag down the bottom window frame to make the window larger. Or you can make the directory-tree portion of the window wider. We'll look at two methods of adjusting the width of the window allocated to the directory tree and file lists.

Dictionary-style thumbing

To scroll quickly in a directory file list, activate the list by clicking any file in it, and then type the first letter of the name of the file you want to find. File Manager scrolls the window to display and select the first name in the list that starts with that letter. For example, typing *n* brings the first file whose name begins with *N* into view. You can also use this method to scroll through the directory tree.

Keyboard navigation

Using the arrow keys is another quick way to scroll up and down through the directory tree. And pressing Enter alternately collapses and expands portions of the directory tree.

Moving up the directory

An up-arrow icon appears at the top of all directory file lists except the root directory. Double-clicking this icon takes you to the directory one level above the one that you're currently viewing and displays the files in that directory.

Adjusting window widths

1. Choose Split from the View menu. A black bar called the split bar appears, spanning the height of the window.
2. Drag the split bar to the right to make the directory tree wider, and click the mouse button.

Or use the mouse to move the split bar:

1. Move the pointer anywhere on the bar that divides the directory tree and the file list. The pointer changes to a pair of horizontal arrows.
2. Drag the split bar to the left to return the directory tree to its original size.

You can also use the file list in the right side of the window to display different directories, as follows:

1. Double-click the SYSTEM folder icon in the file list. Notice that you can display the contents of any subdirectory by double-clicking its folder icon in either the directory tree or the file list.

Moving up one directory level

2. Double-click the upward-pointing arrow icon at the top of the SYSTEM directory's file list. File Manager moves back up in the directory structure to the WINDOWS directory and displays its contents again.

Opening shortcut

To open a document in another application on a one-time-only basis using File Manager, drag the document's icon over to the application's icon, and release the mouse button. The application starts and then attempts to open the document. For example, if you drag a Notepad document's icon to the Write icon, the document opens in a Write window.

Associating extensions

Most documents created by Windows applications are automatically associated with that application. If you want a Windows application to open a document created by a different application or that has an extension you assigned, you must create an association between the application and the extension.

To permanently associate a particular extension with an application, click a file with that extension, and choose Associate from the File menu. Type the name of the application with which you want to associate the extension, and click OK. The application must be able to open or convert that particular type of document for the association to work. For example, you can't open a Lotus 1-2-3 spreadsheet in Aldus PageMaker. If you try, PageMaker displays an error message and opens an untitled, empty window.

Starting Programs from File Manager

In addition to helping you organize directories and files, File Manager allows you to start programs from its directory windows, just as you can from group windows in Program Manager. For example, in Chapter 2, you started Notepad by double-clicking its icon in the Program Manager window. Follow these steps to see how you can start the same program from File Manager:

1. Scroll the WINDOWS directory file list until you can see the icon for NOTEPAD.EXE.
2. Double-click the NOTEPAD.EXE icon. File Manager starts Notepad and displays a blank Notepad window.
3. Close Notepad by choosing Close from the Control menu in the top-left corner of the Notepad window.

As in Program Manager, double-clicking a document icon in File Manager both opens the document and starts the application that created it. Try the following:

1. Locate any file with a BMP extension, and double-click it. Windows starts the file's originating program, Paintbrush, and loads the file—a bitmap graphic.
2. Close Paintbrush by choosing Exit from the File menu.

Organizing Directories and Files

Being able to start programs from File Manager is convenient, but the real strength of File Manager becomes apparent when you use it to organize your directories and files by moving, copying, and deleting them. Performing these operations by typing DOS commands is tedious and error prone. Not only do you have to pick the right command but you have to specify the right parameters in the right order—and type everything without a single mistake. By using a visual interface to make common DOS operations less intimidating, Windows File Manager is in good company; this technique is also used by the DOS Shell released with MS-DOS 5 and by commercial shell programs such as Norton Commander.

Before you practice using File Manager to create directories and move files, you might want to make a few decisions about what you want your directory and file structure to look like. If you have ever wasted time trying to locate a file, you will probably find that spending a few minutes now deciding how to avoid such incidents in the future will more than repay you in increased efficiency.

Deciding on a System

There are no hard and fast rules for organizing files, and the scheme you come up with will depend on the nature of your work. For example, the files created by CityRock Gym (the sports club introduced in Chapter 2) are client-based, so it makes sense to identify the gym's files by client. CityRock might use a client's initials as the first two or three characters of the filename of every file connected with that account, follow these letters with a date, and use the extension to identify the type of file. For greatest flexibility, a file-naming system should use all eight characters allowed by DOS and should always use the same character to pad out empty spaces. The underscore (_) is a good choice. Thus, a filename like RJ052192.LET might designate a letter written to a client whose initials are RJ on May 21, 1992, whereas the filename RJ060392.INV might designate an invoice sent to the same client a few weeks later.

Naming files

The important thing is to come up with a simple scheme and to apply it consistently. In an eagerness to impose structure, people sometimes go overboard, developing convoluted naming systems and subdirectory mazes in which it is easy to get lost. The result is usually as bad as no system at all, because it is less hassle to create filenames on the fly and search a huge directory than it is to remember how the system works.

Advantage of deciding on a system

The advantage of a little file-naming discipline becomes apparent when you accumulate so many files in one directory that you need to create subdirectories to make the files more manageable. For example, suppose CityRock Gym decides to organize their files by type rather than by client. They could create a subdirectory called INVOICES, select all the files in the large directory that have INV as their extension, and move all their invoice files with one command.

It's definitely worth coming up with a few simple rules for organizing directories and files and then training yourself to apply them consistently. You can then use File Manager to manipulate the files, both individually and in groups, as you'll see in the next section.

Creating a New Directory

Although you can easily scroll the WINDOWS directory file list and even jump around in the list of files by typing letters on the keyboard, you might want to organize the WINDOWS directory to make it easier to find specific files. As you scroll the window, notice that the names of files that come with Windows follow a definite pattern. You might not know exactly what a file is or does, but you can tell that certain files relate to specific Windows programs (such as Program Manager) because they have the same filename (such as PROGMAN). Other files probably perform similar functions because they have the same extension.

As a demonstration, we're going to create a new subdirectory for all the bitmap and sound files—those with BMP and WAV as their extensions. The bitmap files can be used as "wallpaper" for the Windows desktop, and the sound files can be used to assign sounds to system events (providing you have the correct sound equipment). They are somewhat extraneous, and moving them into their own subdirectory won't affect the way Windows performs right now. So follow these steps:

1. First, make the WINDOWS directory active by clicking its icon in the directory tree, and then choose the Create Directory command from the File menu. File Manager displays this Create Directory dialog box so that you can give the directory a name:

The Create Directory command

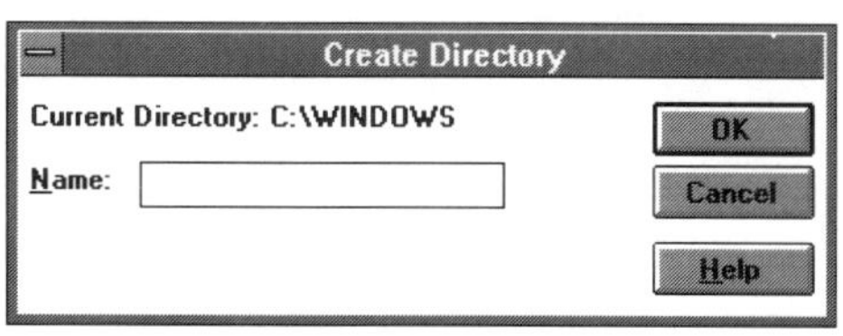

2. Check that the current directory is C:\WINDOWS. Then in the Name text box, type *extra*, and click OK. A new EXTRA folder icon appears both in the directory tree and in the file list, as shown here:

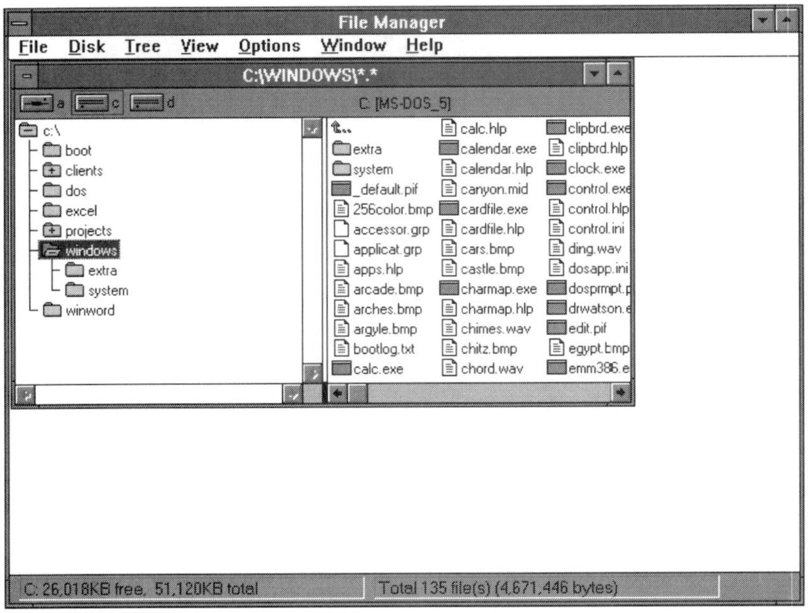

Having created the new directory, we're ready to select the files we want to move into it. Here are the steps:

Selecting files

1. Again, be sure that the WINDOWS directory window is active. Then choose Select Files from the File menu. File Manager displays this dialog box so that you can specify the files you want to select from the file list:

Selecting types of files

To select all files of a certain type, choose By File Type from the View menu, and enter the extension of the file type in the Name text box. For example, to select bitmap files, enter *.BMP, and then click OK. File Manager displays in the file list the names of all the bitmap files in the current directory.

The Search command

The Search command on the File menu can help you track down elusive files. Enter the filename in the Search For text box and where to search in the Start From text box. Enter only the drive letter and choose the Search All Subdirectories option to search the entire hard disk. You can use wildcards in the Search For text box. For example, you can enter **.doc* to search for all Microsoft Word for Windows documents. The results of the search are displayed in the Search Results dialog box, which lists the files in the same way as a directory window. You can then move, copy, and delete these files as a group.

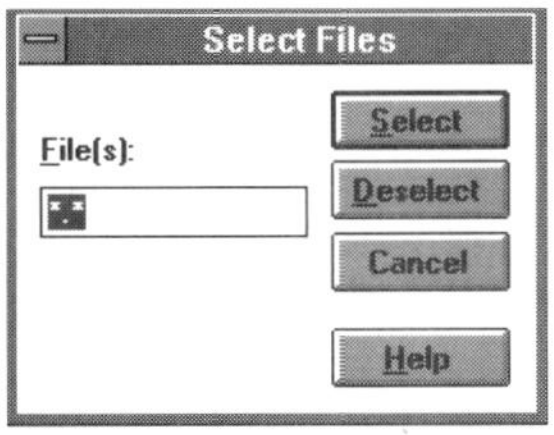

Notice that by default all filenames (represented by *) and all extensions (represented by .*) will be selected. You can restrict the selection of files to those with certain characters in their names or in their extensions by changing this default setting. For this example, you want to select files with the extensions BMP and WAV.

2. Click an insertion point at the end of the setting in the Files text box, and press Backspace to delete the second *.
3. Type *bmp*, and click Select. The Select Files dialog box remains on the screen, and the BMP files appear with a border around them in the files list. At the bottom of the File Manager window, the number of selected files and their total size is displayed.
4. In the Files text box, highlight BMP, type WAV, and click Select. The number of selected files and their size increases to include the WAV files.
5. Click Close. When the dialog box closes, the selected files are highlighted.

Another way of selecting

To select files that are not adjacent in a list of files, click the first file, and then hold down the Ctrl key and click the next file. Continue holding down Ctrl and clicking the files you want, until they are all selected. To deselect just one file from a group of selected files, hold down the Ctrl key, and click the file you want to deselect.

Confirmation settings

Choose Confirmation from the Options menu if you want to change any of File Manager's confirmation settings. For example, you might want to disable settings that are inconvenient, such as Confirm On Mouse Action. When this setting is turned off, File Manager no longer asks for confirmation of mouse actions like moving and copying files.

Now for the move, which you can accomplish in two ways: using the Move command on the File menu or using the mouse. Here, we'll use the mouse, which is faster but requires a bit more precision. (In the following steps, be careful not to click anywhere other than on the selected files, because clicking elsewhere will deselect the files. If you click accidentally, use the Select Files dialog box to select the files again.) This is what you do:

Moving files

1. Click any one of the highlighted files. Then hold down the mouse button. The pointer changes to a stack-of-documents icon. Drag this icon to the EXTRA directory's folder icon in either the file list or the directory tree. When the pointer is in the correct spot over the EXTRA folder icon, File Manager surrounds the icon with a border.
2. Release the mouse button. File Manager displays this dialog box to verify that you want to move the files:

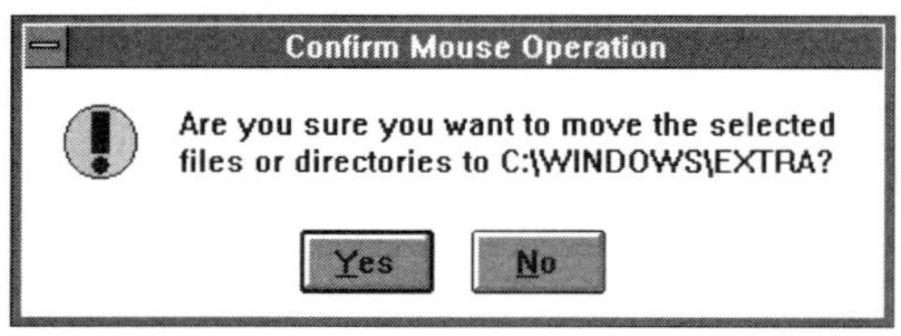

3. Click Yes to confirm the mouse action. File Manager moves all the selected files from the WINDOWS directory into the EXTRA directory, displaying the move operation's progress in a message box. When the program has moved the files, it closes the message box.
4. Click the EXTRA folder icon in the directory tree to display its files in the file list, and verify that the BMP and WAV files are safely stored in their new directory.

The File menu

If you are wary of using the mouse to manipulate files and directories, you'll find commands on the File menu that perform the same tasks. Simply select the file or directory, and choose the command. Some commands, like Rename, Properties, and Search, perform tasks you can't do with the mouse. (You use Properties to set attributes, such as read-only.)

Moving, Copying, and Deleting Directories

Moving a directory using DOS commands is a multistep, confusing process that involves first copying the directory and then deleting it. In File Manager, you move directories just as you move files—by dragging them. Try this:

1. In the directory tree, be sure that the WINDOWS directory is still expanded to show its subdirectories.

Moving directories

2. Click the EXTRA directory, hold down the mouse button, and drag the icon that appears toward the C:\ directory at the top of the tree. When the pointer is in the correct spot over the C:\ folder icon, File Manager surrounds the icon with a border.

3. Release the mouse button. When File Manager displays the confirmation dialog box, click Yes. File Manager then moves the EXTRA directory to the root directory, displaying the operation's progress in a message box. When the program has moved the directory, it closes the dialog box.

In File Manager, dragging a directory (or a file) to a new location on the same drive always moves the directory. To copy a directory instead of moving it, you hold down the Ctrl key while dragging. Try these steps:

Copying directories

1. Hold down the Ctrl key, and drag the EXTRA directory icon over to the WINDOWS directory icon in the directory tree. If you can't see the WINDOWS directory icon, drag the bottom border of the directory window to enlarge it. (Remember, you can also collapse extraneous subdirectories by double-clicking directory icons that have minus symbols.)

2. Click Yes when File Manager asks you to confirm the copy operation. As it copies, File Manager displays the operation's progress in a message box. When it is through copying, you see one EXTRA directory in the WINDOWS directory and another EXTRA directory in the root directory, as shown here:

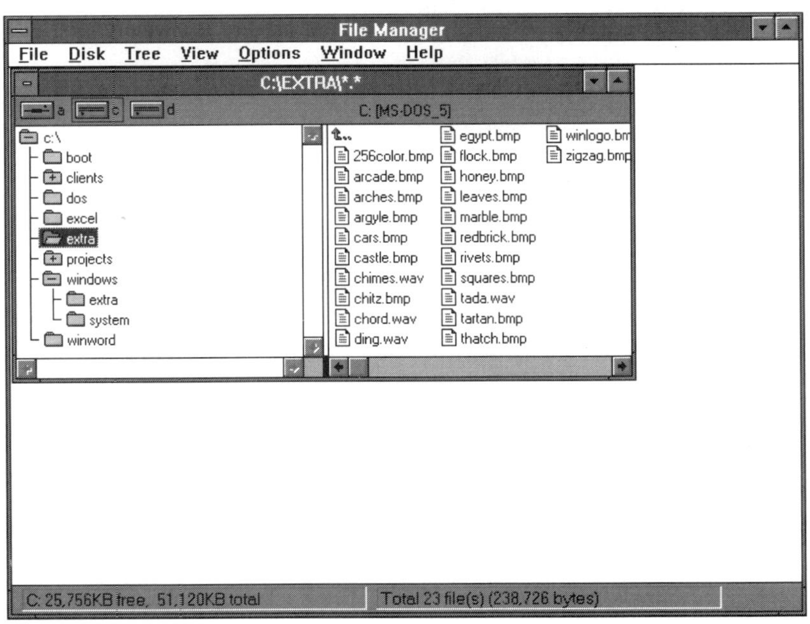

You don't need two copies of the EXTRA directory, so let's delete one of them:

Deleting directories

1. Click the icon of the EXTRA directory in the C:\ directory to select it.
2. Press the Del key, or choose Delete from the File menu. Either way, File Manager displays this dialog box:

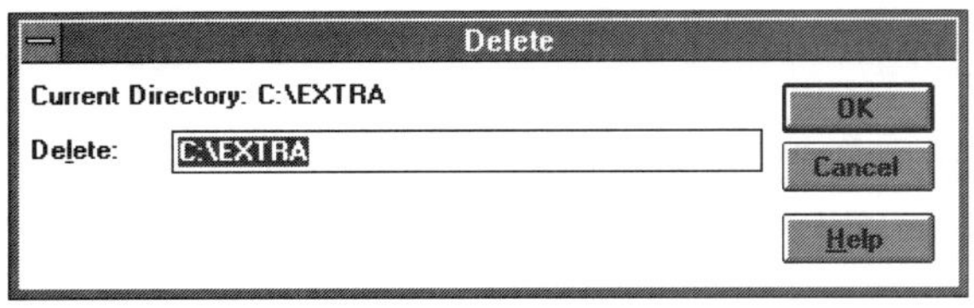

3. Click OK. File Manager displays this message box:

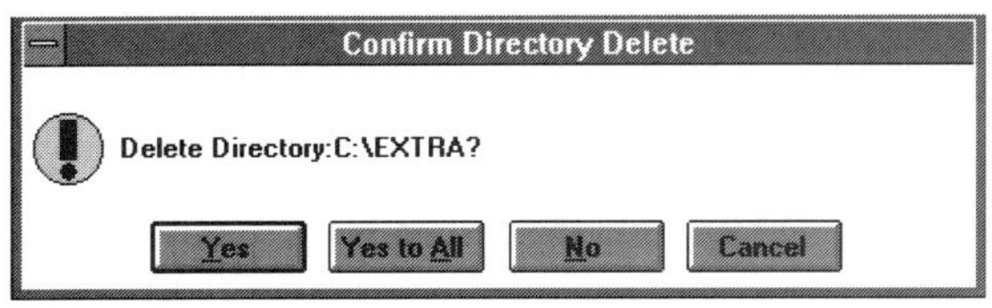

4. Click Yes. File Manager then asks you to confirm that you want to delete the first file in the directory. If you click Yes again, File Manager will continue asking for confirmation before deleting each file in the directory.
5. To tell File Manager to go ahead and delete all the files in the directory, click Yes To All. File Manager deletes all the files and then deletes the EXTRA directory.

Copying Files to a Floppy Disk

Suppose you are running out of room on your hard disk and you are looking for files to remove in order to give yourself a little breathing space. For example, CityRock Gym might decide to remove all the invoice files for 1991, and they would almost certainly want to copy the files to archival storage on a floppy disk before erasing them. If they have named all their invoice files consistently with filenames such as RJ120491.INV, as we discussed earlier in the chapter, copying the files for 1991 is simple. They would first select all the files with filenames ending in 91 that have INV extensions by choosing the Select Files command from the File menu, typing *??????91.INV* in the Files text box, and then clicking Select and Close. Then they would copy the selected files to a floppy disk.

On your system, you may not have a set of files with which you can practice copying files to a floppy disk, so use the bitmap and sound files that you just moved into the EXTRA directory as you follow these steps:

1. In the directory tree, click the EXTRA directory icon to display its contents.
2. Choose the New Window command from the Window menu to display a second directory window.

Displaying another directory window

3. Expand the File Manager window (*not* the directory window) by clicking the Maximize button in the top-right corner of the window. Then tidy up the window by choosing Tile from the Window menu. Now the two directory windows each take up half the File Manager window. Notice that drive icons appear at the top of each window.
4. Insert a blank, formatted floppy disk in drive A, and click the A drive icon at the top of one of the windows. Your screen changes to look like the one at the top of the next page. As you can see, the root directory for the floppy disk appears in the directory tree portion of that window, and the message *No Files Found* appears in the file list. The status bar at the bottom of the File Manager window displays information about the floppy-disk drive.

The Refresh command

You might notice that File Manager updates the file list when you copy files from one directory to another. But if you display the file list for a floppy drive and then switch floppy disks, you'll need to manually update the file list by choosing Refresh from the Window menu. You might also need to use Refresh to update the file list for a network drive.

A memory for directories

If you don't like cluttering up the screen with multiple windows and icons, you can trust File Manager to remember the last active directory when copying files to a different drive. For example, suppose you are working in File Manager and you open the WINDOWS directory on drive C. If you then activate drive D, select some files, and drag them to the C drive icon, File Manager copies the files to the WINDOWS directory, not the C:\ directory, as you might expect.

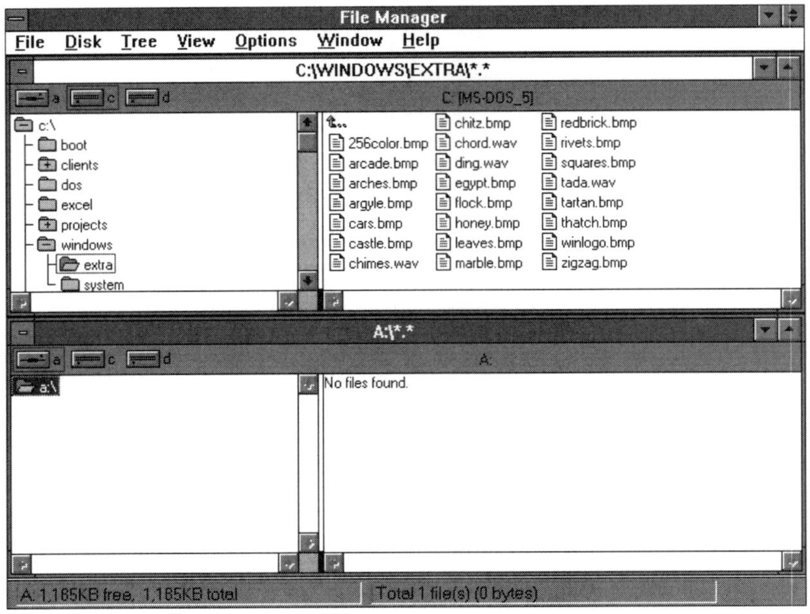

5. Select the EXTRA directory in the other directory window (scroll the directory tree if necessary).

Selecting files

6. Select all the files in the directory, using one of three methods: Use the Select Files command as described earlier; click one of the files to activate the file list, and then press Ctrl+/ (forward slash); or click the first file in the list, hold down Shift, and click the last file in the list (File Manager selects all the files, from the first through the last).

7. Click one of the selected files, drag the stack-of-documents icon over to the A drive's directory window, and release the mouse button.

8. Click Yes when File Manager asks you to confirm the copy operation. File Manager begins copying files from the EXTRA directory to the disk in drive A, reporting on the operation's progress in a message box. When File Manager has finished copying the files, they appear in the A drive's directory window, as shown at the top of the next page.

Moving files to a different directory

For demonstration purposes, we opened two windows to copy the files from the hard disk to the root directory of the floppy disk. Usually, you will use this technique to copy and move files between different directories on your hard drive, or to a specific directory on a floppy disk. To move files to the root directory of a floppy disk, you can simply select the files and

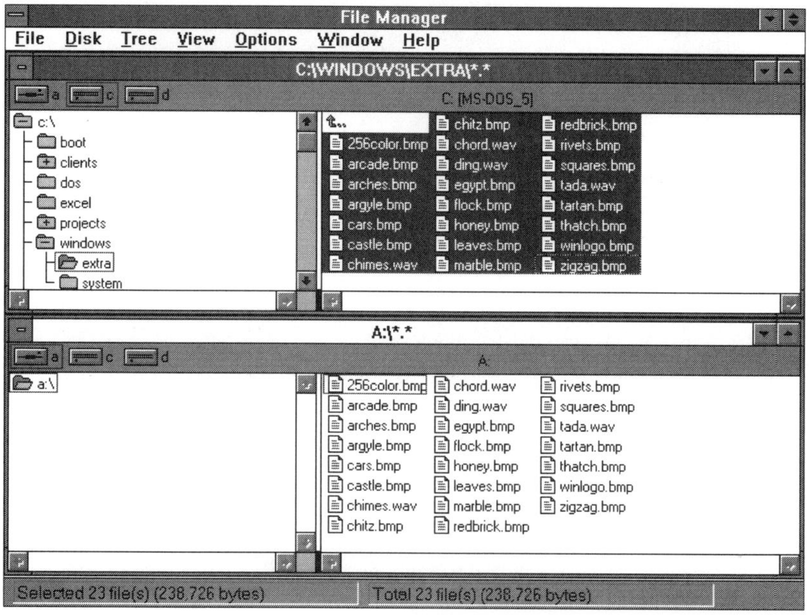

then hold down the Shift key while you drag the stack-of-documents icon directly to the A drive icon at the top of the directory window. As a safety measure, however, we recommend that you copy your files first and then delete them from your hard disk, rather than moving them.

Copying Files from a Floppy Disk

Now that you know how to quickly copy files from your hard disk to a floppy disk, you'll want to know how to use File Manager to copy them back to your hard disk. Again, we'll use the bitmap and sound files to demonstrate. This time, we'll copy the files back to the WINDOWS directory where they belong. Both directory windows from the previous example should still be open on your screen. If they aren't, open them before following these steps:

1. Select the WINDOWS directory in the C drive's directory tree.

Shrinking directory windows to icons

2. Click the Minimize button in the top-right corner of the WINDOWS directory window. Then click the Minimize button of the A drive directory window. As you can see on the next page, the directory windows shrink down to icons at the bottom of the File Manager window, just as group windows shrink down to icons at the bottom of the Program Manager window.

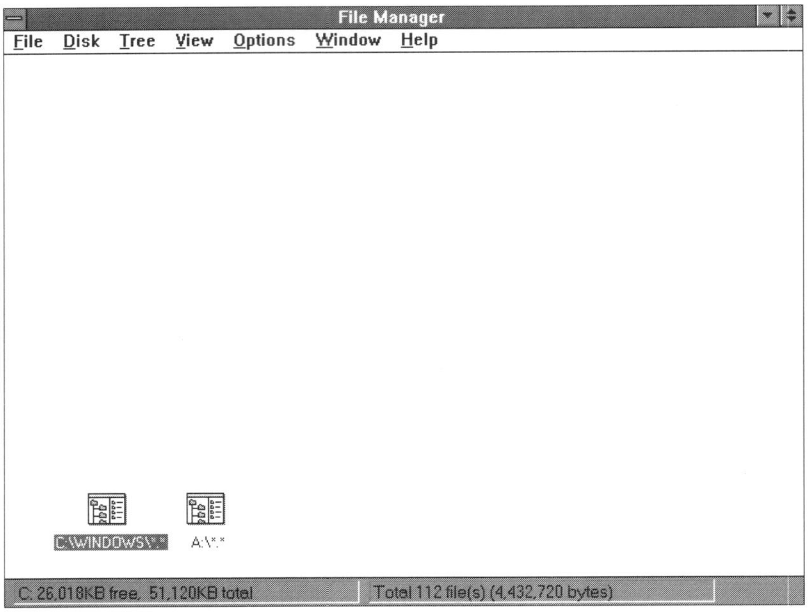

Beneath the icons are the paths to the active directories. Keeping commonly used directories as icons at the bottom of the window is a handy way of jumping from directory to directory, as well as copying or moving files. If the Save Settings On Exit command on the Options menu is active when you exit File Manager, these icons will be present the next time you start File Manager.

3. Click the A drive directory icon once to pop up its Control menu, and then choose Restore.

Formatting floppy disks

In File Manager, you can format floppy disks, and even make bootable system disks, without quitting to DOS. Simply insert a disk in your floppy-disk drive, and choose Format Disk from the Disk menu. In the Format Disk dialog box, select a floppy drive from the Disk In drop-down list, and then select a disk capacity from the Capacity drop-down list. Select the Make System Disk option if you want the disk to be a bootable DOS disk—a disk that contains the files necessary to boot your computer and start DOS. Select the Quick Format option to reformat previously formatted disks. Enter a name in the Label text box if you want to name the disk. Then click OK. Click Yes when File Manager asks you to confirm that you want to format the disk. When File Manager has finished the formatting operation, it asks whether you want to format another disk. Click Yes to format another disk or No to quit.

If you simply want to turn an already formatted disk into a bootable DOS disk, choose Make System Disk from the Disk menu in the File Manager window.

4. Move the restored window out of the way so that you can see the WINDOWS directory icon.
5. Select all the files on the floppy disk, drag the stack-of-documents icon to the WINDOWS directory icon, and release the mouse button. Answer Yes when File Manager asks you to confirm the copy.
6. Close the A drive directory window by choosing Close from its Control menu, and then restore the WINDOWS directory window by double-clicking it. The bitmap files and the sound files are all back in the WINDOWS directory file list, where they belong.

Now you can delete the EXTRA directory, as follows:

1. Select the EXTRA directory icon in the directory tree, and press Del.
2. Click OK in the Delete dialog box, and click Yes in the Confirm Directory Delete dialog box.
3. In the Confirm File Delete dialog box, click Yes To All to delete all the sound and bitmap files.
4. If you want, delete the copies of the sound and bitmap files that are on the floppy disk.

Move vs. copy

As we mentioned earlier, if you want to move files to a different *drive* rather than copy them, you must hold down the Shift key while you drag the stack-of-documents icon, because File Manager's default action is to *copy* the files from one drive to another. However, when you drag the stack-of-documents icon from one *directory* to another on the same drive, as you did when you moved the bitmap and sound files from the WINDOWS directory to the EXTRA directory, File Manager's default action is to *move* the files, so you need to hold down the Ctrl key while dragging if you want to *copy* the files instead.

In this chapter, we have shown you a few basic file operations that will make your work with Windows more productive. In the next chapter, we look at more Windows techniques for improving efficiency: multitasking and sharing information among programs.

4 Switching and Sharing

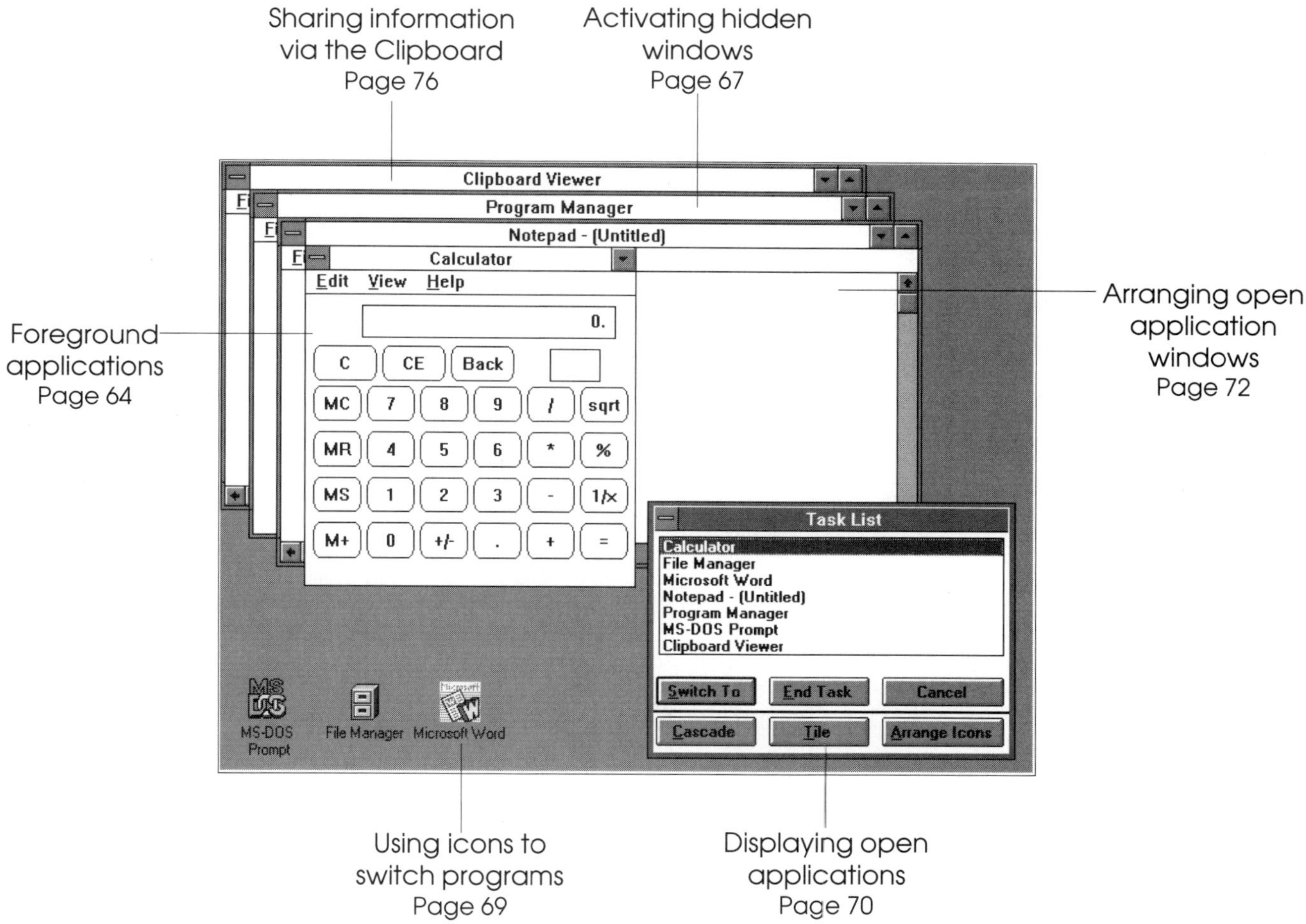
Sharing information via the Clipboard Page 76
Activating hidden windows Page 67
Foreground applications Page 64
Arranging open application windows Page 72
Using icons to switch programs Page 69
Displaying open applications Page 70
Clipboard Viewer
Program Manager
Notepad - (Untitled)
Calculator
Edit View Help
Task List
Calculator
File Manager
Microsoft Word
Notepad - (Untitled)
Program Manager
MS-DOS Prompt
Clipboard Viewer
Switch To
End Task
Cancel
Cascade
Tile
Arrange Icons
MS-DOS Prompt
File Manager
Microsoft Word

Perhaps the single most important Windows feature is its ability to run more than one program at a time. Although being able to group programs visually and organize files logically will undoubtedly increase your efficiency, multitasking will probably be one of your main reasons for working in the Windows environment.

In Chapters 2 and 3, you got a feel for moving among open windows and copying information from one window to another. In this chapter, we cover switching from one program to another and sharing information among programs in more detail. After you read this chapter, you'll begin to see how to take advantage of having a variety of programs at your fingertips all at the same time.

Multitasking Techniques

The term *multitasking* might sound intimidating, but the concept is simple: Multitasking is running more than one program at the same time. For example, you might use the Terminal program to download a file from an online service while using the Notepad program to jot down notes for a meeting with a client. No longer do you have to wait for the communications program to finish before you can use your computer for other work. The extent to which you can multitask depends on the mode in which you are running Windows, but both modes allow some degree of multitasking between Windows applications. (We talk about the two Windows modes in detail on page 73.)

Foreground applications

Background applications

Although you can have more than one program running at the same time, only one program can run *in the foreground*, meaning that its window is active and receiving input from you. Any other open programs run *in the background*, meaning that they are busy behind the scenes, either carrying out some prescribed task or waiting for your next instruction.

To see the difference between foreground and background applications, let's go back to CityRock Gym in Emeryville, California. Suppose Peter Mayfield wants to calculate the total number of hours worked the previous week by the staff at the Gym. Follow along with these steps:

1. If you have moved on to this chapter from Chapter 3, close all open windows except the Program Manager window.

2. Be sure the Program Manager window is maximized so that it fills the screen. Double-click the icon for the group in which Notepad is stored (the Word Processing group if you have been following along with the examples; the Accessories group if you haven't been following along). Then double-click the Notepad icon to start Notepad and display an empty Notepad document.

3. Type the names of the staff members—*Hanneli, Amy, David, Bill, Mike*, and *Robin*—pressing Enter after each name. Your screen looks like this:

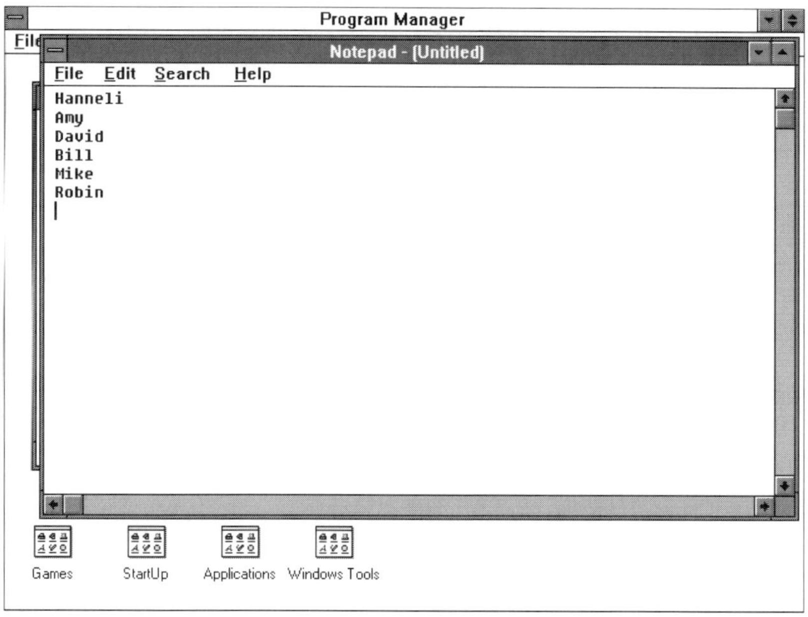

4. Click anywhere on the Program Manager window to activate it. Because the Notepad window is no longer active, and because the Program Manager window is maximized, the Notepad window disappears into the background. But Notepad is still running, and although you can't see it, the document with the list of staff names is still open.

Starting Calculator

5. Double-click the icon for the group where the Calculator is stored (the Windows Tools group if you have been following along with the examples; the Accessories group if you haven't

been following along). Then double-click the Calculator icon to start the Windows Calculator program. The image of a standard calculator appears on the screen.

Quick addition

6. Add the hours worked last week by the first staff member. For this example, click the 5 key, and then click the + key. Next, click the 4 key and +. Click 4 and + again. Then click 6 and +. Finally, click 8 and +. The display bar now contains 27, the total:

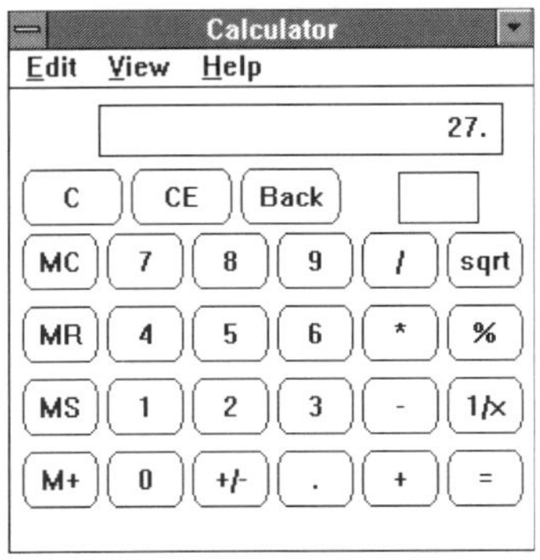

Copying from one program

7. Choose Copy from the Edit menu. Calculator copies the contents of its display bar to the Clipboard.

Now you need to paste the total in the Notepad document. But where is the Notepad window, and how do you activate it? Here's how:

1. Hold down Alt, and press Esc. The Calculator window closes.

Loading files into Notepad

Notepad can load unformatted ASCII files up to 50 KB in size. If lines of text go beyond the right border of a Notepad window, activate Word Wrap on the Edit menu so that all the text appears in the window. Turning on Word Wrap is for display purposes only; it doesn't affect the text file in any way.

Entering numbers

You can use the keyboard instead of the mouse to enter numbers into Calculator. Just press the NumLock key on your keyboard and use the numeric keypad to enter numbers and operators. (In this case, the Enter key on the numeric keypad functions like the = button on the Calculator.)

The Scientific Calculator

Choosing Scientific from the View menu turns Calculator into a powerful, full-featured scientific/programmer's calculator. The basic algebraic functions remain, but you can also use this calculator to perform many different scientific and statistical calculations in either hexadecimal, decimal, octal, or binary number systems.

Activating hidden windows

2. Press Alt+Esc again. Notepad comes to the foreground, with the staff-names document open.
3. Move the pointer to just after the first staff member's name, and click the mouse button to create an insertion point.

Pasting into another program

4. Press the Tab key, and choose Paste from the Edit menu. The Calculator's total, 27, is pasted into the Notepad document, as shown here:

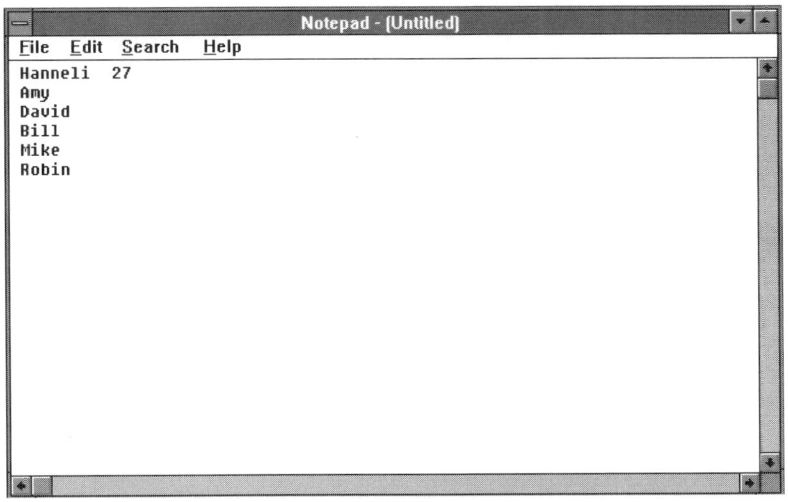

Now you need to go back to the Calculator to total the second staff member's hours:

1. Press Alt+Esc to activate Calculator, and add up the hours for Amy (for practice, just make them up). Then choose Copy to put the total on the Clipboard.

Running multiple copies of an application

Some applications can run several "copies" of themselves. For example, you could run a Standard Calculator as well as a Scientific Calculator, or run several Notepads, sharing information among them. To run multiple copies of an application, start the program as you would normally, and then simply start it again.

Alt+Esc and Alt+Tab

Pressing Alt+Esc brings open programs to the foreground one at a time, in the order in which you opened them. To find a program without bringing any others to the foreground, hold down the Alt key and press Tab. If you keep the Alt key down, Windows displays a dialog box with the next open program's name and its icon. Keep pressing Tab until you find the application you want, and then release the Alt key to bring it to the foreground.

2. Press Alt+Esc twice to bring Notepad to the foreground, click an insertion point after Amy's name, press the Tab key, and choose Paste to enter her total hours.

Finding Background Programs

When several programs are running at once, you might forget that a particular program is already running and double-click the program's icon in its group window to start it again. Usually, Windows reports that the program is already running and tells you that you can run the program only once. However, some programs, such as Notepad, start a new copy of the program with a blank document each time you double-click their icons. Each copy of the program consumes memory, and multiple copies of the same program can make it harder to find what you want when you want it.

If you want to check whether a program is already running or if you have trouble locating a specific program, you can cycle through all the open programs by pressing Alt+Esc. However, Windows provides an easy way to see at a glance which programs are running in the background. Try this:

1. Press Alt+Esc until the Program Manager window is active.
2. Click the Minimize button in the Program Manager window. (You can also choose Minimize from the window's Control menu.) The Program Manager window shrinks to an icon at the bottom of the screen, and Windows displays the windows of the programs that are running in the background—in this case, Notepad and Calculator.

Displaying background windows

3. Click the Calculator window, and use Calculator to total the hours of the third staff member, alternately clicking five numbers and the + key. Then choose Copy.
4. Click the Notepad window. Instead of disappearing, the Calculator window moves behind the Notepad window. (You might have to shrink the Notepad window to see Calculator.)
5. Click an insertion point after the third staff member's name, press the Tab key, and choose Paste to enter his total hours.

Minimizing Running Programs

You can minimize the windows of running programs so that they are represented by icons at the bottom of the screen. If you minimize a program while the Program Manager window is maximized, the program's icon disappears behind the Program Manager window. But when Program Manager is also minimized, the program's icon is easy to spot, and you can double-click it to switch to that program. Try this:

1. Click the Minimize button in the top-right corner of the Notepad window. The window shrinks to an icon and moves to the bottom of the screen. The Calculator window is now active.
2. Use Calculator to total the fourth staff member's hours, choose Copy, and then click the Calculator window's Minimize button to shrink the window to an icon.
3. Now double-click the Notepad icon. The icon expands to display the document window.

   Using icons to switch programs
4. Click an insertion point after the fourth staff member's name, press the Tab key, and choose Paste to enter his total hours.
5. Click the Notepad window's Minimize button to send the window back to the bottom of the screen as an icon.
6. Double-click the Calculator icon to display Calculator, total the fifth staff member's hours, choose Copy, and click the Minimize button.
7. Activate Notepad, click an insertion point after the fifth staff member's name, press the Tab key, choose Paste to enter his total hours, and click the Minimize button.

Using Task Manager

The techniques for finding and activating programs that we have just discussed work well when you are running only a few applications at one time. However, when you are running many applications, especially non-Windows applications, you need a more efficient way of switching among them. Windows anticipates this need by providing a feature called Task Manager.

Activating Programs from the Task List You can access Task Manager by choosing the Switch To command, which is found on the Control menus of most program windows. Choosing Switch To opens the Task List window, which lists all the programs that are currently running. Switching from one to another is then a simple matter of selecting the program you want to activate. Try using Task Manager to switch between Notepad and Calculator:

1. Double-click the Program Manager icon to open its window.

Displaying open applications

2. Choose Switch To from the Control menu in the top-left corner of the Program Manager window to display a Task List like this one:

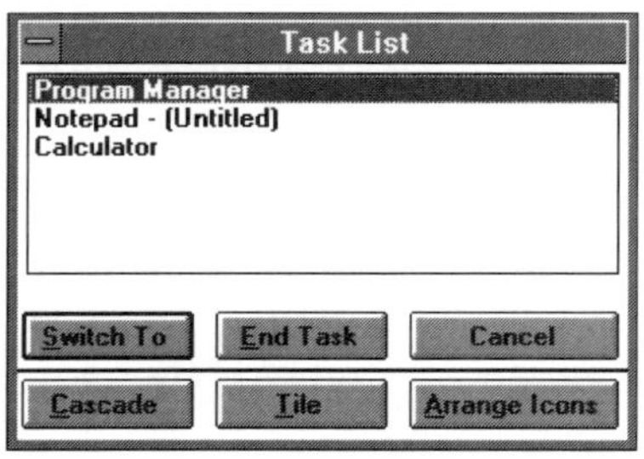

The open applications appear in the list box, with the active application—Program Manager—at the top of the list. The other two programs we are running—Notepad and Calculator—are listed below it.

3. Click Calculator, and then click the Switch To button to activate the Calculator window.

4. Use Calculator to total the hours for the sixth staff member, Robin, and then choose Copy.

5. Choose Switch To from Calculator's Control menu to display the Task List, and click first Notepad and then the Switch To button, or double-click Notepad. The Calculator window is replaced by the Notepad window.

6. In the Notepad window, click an insertion point after Robin's name, press the Tab key, and then choose Paste to enter her total hours.

7. Click anywhere in the Program Manager window. Notepad moves to the background.

Quitting Programs from the Task List Using Task Manager, you can quit an open application without first switching to that program. To quit Calculator and Notepad:

1. Choose Switch To from the Program Manager's Control menu, and click Calculator to select it.
2. Click the End Task button. Windows closes both the program and the Task List window.
3. Choose Switch To again. This time click Notepad, and then click the End Task button. Because you have not yet saved the open Notepad document, Windows brings the Notepad window to the foreground and displays the dialog box shown below:

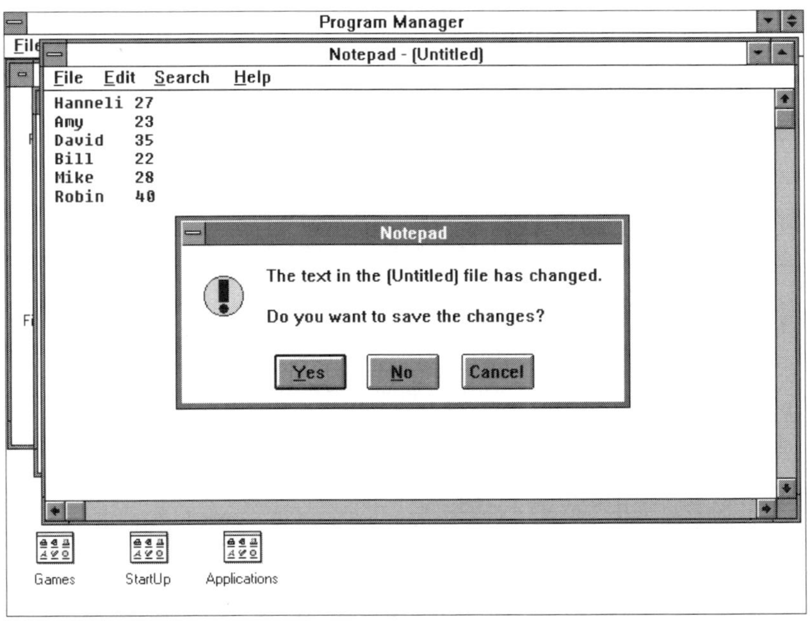

4. Click Yes. Windows displays the Save As dialog box so that you can specify a filename.
5. Type a name like HR042492.TXT (for *hours for the week ending April 24, 1992*) in the Filename text box, and click OK. Windows closes the document, Notepad, and the Task List window.

Quitting Non-Windows Applications In 386 Enhanced mode, you cannot quit a non-Windows application by clicking the End Task button. You must exit the application the way you normally do when running it from DOS. If you are running Windows in Standard mode, when you click End Task to close a non-Windows application from the Task List window, Windows can't tell whether the application's active file has been saved, so it always displays a warning. If you are certain that you have saved the application's active file, simply click OK in the message box to close the application. You lose any unsaved files when the application closes.

Arranging Windows and Icons The Task List window has Cascade, Tile, and Arrange Icons buttons that work similarly to the commands with the same names on Program Manager's Window menu. (We discussed these commands in Chapter 2). The only difference is that the buttons affect all application windows and icons, whether they are running in the foreground or the background, except non-Windows applications that are running full screen (see page 74 for more information about these applications).

Cascading windows

Tiling windows

Clicking Cascade in the Task List window causes all open application windows (including Program Manager) to overlap so that the title bar of each window is visible. Clicking Tile arranges and sizes the windows so that none of them overlap. (Some windows, like the Calculator window, cannot

Task Manager and non-Windows applications

A full-screen non-Windows application has no Control menu, so you can't choose Switch To to access the Task List. However, you can still use the Ctrl+Esc shortcut. Windows switches to Program Manager and opens the Task List window. To return to the application, simply double-click its name in the Task List window or double-click its icon at the bottom of the screen.

Complete Task List

If you are running more than one copy of the same program, each copy is listed in the Task List window, so you can, for example, select between an open Standard Calculator and an open Scientific Calculator. In addition, any open Windows-application documents are also listed, so you can select between documents open in two copies of a program like Notepad.

Task Manager shortcut

Double-click any empty area of the desktop to display the Task List dialog box. Or press Ctrl+Esc. Remember, the desktop is the area behind all open windows and icons. If the Program Manager window is maximized, you can't see the desktop.

be resized. As a result, the Tile and Cascade options cannot arrange them as neatly as other windows.) Clicking Arrange Icons arranges all open application icons neatly across the bottom of the screen. Note that these three buttons do not affect windows and icons within the Program Manager window; they affect the Program Manager window as a whole.

Windows Two Modes

Windows 3.1 can run in two modes: Standard and 386 Enhanced. Previous versions of Windows offered a third mode, Real mode, which was primarily for PCs and XTs (earlier computer models with 8086 and 8088 chips). Some older Windows applications can run only in Real mode and as a result will not run in Windows 3.1. You might want to consider updating these programs to newer versions to take advantage of the power of Windows 3.1.

Which mode you run in depends primarily on your processor chip and memory configuration. The level of multitasking you can achieve, in turn, depends on which mode you are running in. The mode also affects the way non-Windows applications are handled. When you start Windows by typing *win* at the C> prompt, the program runs by default in the most powerful mode possible. Alternatively, you can start Windows in a specific mode by typing *win* followed by an instruction called a *switch.*

Standard Mode

ATs and PS/2s (which have 80286, 80386, or 80486 chips) with at least 640 KB of conventional memory and 256 KB of extended memory can run Windows in Standard mode. This mode takes advantage of all available system memory, but non-Windows applications are limited to 640 KB of memory (the standard DOS limitation). Type *win /s* to run in Standard mode. Even if your machine can run in 386 Enhanced mode, you might want to run Windows in Standard mode, because this mode is generally faster than 386 Enhanced mode.

Multitasking is possible among Windows applications in Standard mode, but Windows might have to swap information between memory and the hard disk when memory is overloaded. You can run a non-Windows application in Standard mode, but while the application is running, you cannot multitask. When you switch to the non-Windows application, it completely takes over the screen. Any background applications freeze, and background operations are not possible. If you switch to a Windows application or to another non-Windows application, the current non-Windows application is halted.

Full-screen non-Windows applications

386 Enhanced Mode

Computers with the 80386 and 80486 chips and at least 640 KB of conventional memory and 1 MB of extended memory can run Windows in 386 Enhanced mode. If your computer meets these specifications, Windows automatically starts in this mode when you type *win* at the C> prompt. If you have set up your system to automatically run Windows in Standard mode, you can type *win /3* to run in 386 Enhanced mode. You can also use this switch to force Windows to run in 386 Enhanced mode if your computer meets the necessary requirements but you have only 384 KB of extended memory.

When your computer is running Windows in 386 Enhanced mode, it can't run most applications created for Windows 2.0 because they can't take advantage of a memory-management technique, called *virtual memory*, that is used by this mode. The virtual-memory technique allows Windows to use more memory than is physically available by treating disk space as though it is memory. Even non-Windows applications can use virtual memory when running under Windows in this mode.

386 Enhanced mode allows true multitasking and background processing, even among non-Windows applications. You can

Switching non-Windows applications

You can switch among open non-Windows applications by using the same shortcuts you use for Windows applications, Alt+Esc and Alt+Tab. When you use the Alt+Tab shortcut, you will see the next application's name in a bar at the top of a blank screen. Keep pressing Tab until the correct application name appears, and then release the Alt key to switch to the application.

run Windows and non-Windows applications in the background while running either a Windows or a non-Windows application in the foreground. The performance of all open programs might suffer slightly as Windows allocates time "slices" to each program.

You can run non-Windows applications either full screen or in their own windows with a Control menu. The second alternative gives non-Windows applications some of the functionality of Windows applications, including the ability to copy and paste data between applications. You can use the PIF Editor (discussed on page 106) to control many aspects of a non-Windows application's behavior under Windows.

Sharing Information among Applications

Another powerful Windows feature is the ease with which you can share information among applications. Sharing is accomplished by copying and pasting information between applications that use compatible data.

If you have followed along with the examples we've covered so far, you know that sharing information among the programs that come with Windows is easy. Moving information between independent Windows applications, such as Word for Windows and Excel, is equally simple. Just select the data in the application file from which you're copying, choose Copy from the File menu, open the application file in which you want to paste the information, select an insertion point, and choose Paste from the File menu.

Sharing information with a non-Windows application can be more complicated, however, and you use different techniques in Standard mode than those you use in 386 Enhanced mode.

Sharing in Standard Mode

As a rule, our examples are designed to show you how to use a particular Windows feature to accomplish some real task. Because we can't predict which Windows and non-Windows applications you might want to work with, the instructions in the rest of this section are necessarily generic. They are, however, specific enough for you to apply them to the applications you use every day.

Copying from Non-Windows Applications In Standard mode, you can copy only a full screen of text or numbers from non-Windows applications, because all non-Windows applications run full screen in this mode. The copy operation uses a character-based print-screen function, so you can't copy and paste graphics from a non-Windows application in these modes.

To copy a screenful of data from a non-Windows application to an open Windows application, follow these steps:

Copying a screenful of data

1. In the source file in the non-Windows application, display the information you want to copy, and press the PrintScreen key. (On older, non-enhanced keyboards, press Shift+PrtSc.) The characters on the screen are copied to the Clipboard.
2. Press Alt+Esc until the destination document in the Windows application is displayed.
3. Choose Paste from the Edit menu. The full screen—including any menu names, window borders, and so forth—is pasted into the designated file. (You will probably need to delete extraneous characters.)

Mouse limitations

When a non-Windows application is displayed in a window, the mouse does not work as it normally would. It simply acts as a selection tool, and allows you to manipulate the window and the Control menu.

Copying the screen

Copying the screen is a way of sharing charts, drawings, and other images created in a non-Windows application. Press Alt+PrintScreen. The entire window is copied to the Clipboard in bitmap (BMP) format. You can then paste the image into a paint program, manipulate it, and then paste it into another Windows application.

Unrecoverable application errors

If a program is not responding to commands or misbehaves in any way, you can force its window to close by pressing Ctrl+Alt+Del. Windows displays a screen with three choices. Press Esc to return to the same program. Press Enter to close the application and return to Windows. Press Ctrl+Alt+Del to reboot your computer. The last two methods result in loss of unsaved work in closed windows.

Pasting into Non-Windows Applications Pasting into a non-Windows application file is more complex than pasting into a Windows application file. Whether you want to paste information from one non-Windows application to another or from a Windows application to a non-Windows application, you can paste only unformatted text. Other types of data and any text formatting are lost during the paste operation.

With the copied information from the Windows or non-Windows application on the Clipboard, follow these steps to paste the information into a non-Windows application:

1. Switch to the destination file in the non-Windows application, and position the cursor where you want to paste the data.
2. Press Alt+Esc until the icon for the non-Windows application is selected at the bottom of the screen.
3. Click the icon. The application's Control menu pops up.
4. Choose Paste. (In 386 Enhanced mode, choose Paste from the Edit submenu.) Windows switches to the non-Windows application and pastes the data into the destination file. You can now format the data as necessary.

Sharing in 386 Enhanced Mode

In 386 Enhanced mode, you can use the copy and paste techniques just described for Standard mode to share information with a non-Windows application that is running full screen. However, if the application is running in its own window, you can access Control menu commands. As a result, copying data to the application's documents is more like copying between Windows applications. For example, you can copy entire screens as bitmap (BMP) images and paste them into a Windows program such as Paintbrush. You can use this technique to copy a graphic or chart from a non-Windows application to a Windows application.

By default, non-Windows applications run full screen, even in 386 Enhanced mode. To copy selected data or to copy the screen as a bitmap image, you need to run the non-Windows application in a window. Follow the instructions on the next page to temporarily display an application in a window.

1. With the application already running, press Alt+Enter. The application appears in a window with a Control menu.

   If you are working in 386 Enhanced mode, an alternative way of running the application in a window is to switch to Program Manager and click the application's icon at the bottom of the screen to open its Control menu. Then choose Settings, and select the Window option.

   Here's how to specify that the non-Windows application should always run in a window:

1. Open the program's PIF file with PIF Editor.
2. Choose the Windowed option.
3. Save the PIF file.

   (PIFs and PIF Editor are covered in more detail on page 106.)

Working with Windowed Non-Windows Applications

You've seen that non-Windows applications running in windows have Control menus, just like Windows applications. You use this menu to copy data from a windowed non-Windows application, as follows:

Marking data to be copied

1. Choose Edit from the Control menu, and then choose Mark from the Edit submenu, as shown here:

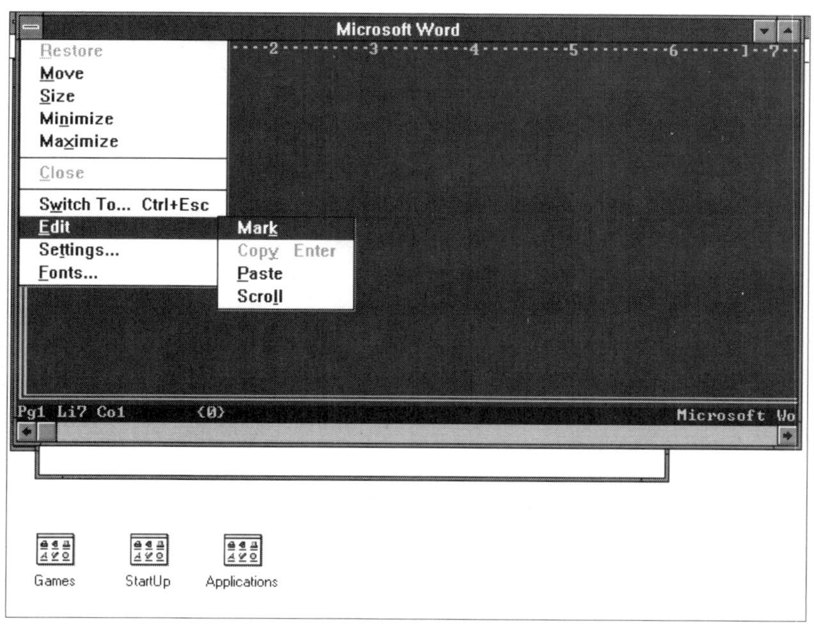

Marking strategy

Mark only the characters you want to copy in a non-Windows program. If your copy area includes window borders or menu names, these items are copied along with the selected text. When pasted into another program, the characters that make up the borders and menus are also pasted in, often as gibberish.

The word *Mark* appears in the application's title bar.

2. Use the mouse to select the data you want to copy by dragging through it. The word *Select* now appears in the title bar.

3. Choose Copy from the Edit submenu to place a copy of the selection on the Clipboard.

4. Switch to the Windows or non-Windows application in which you want to paste the information, position the cursor, and choose Paste from the application's Edit menu or from the Edit submenu.

In this chapter, we've covered some techniques that will make your Windows sessions faster and more productive. Now that you have an idea of the power of multitasking and you know some of the methods of sharing information among applications, we'll move on to discuss the many useful programs that come with Windows. By opening various combinations of programs on your desktop, you can put Windows to maximum use in your daily work.

5 The Windows Tools

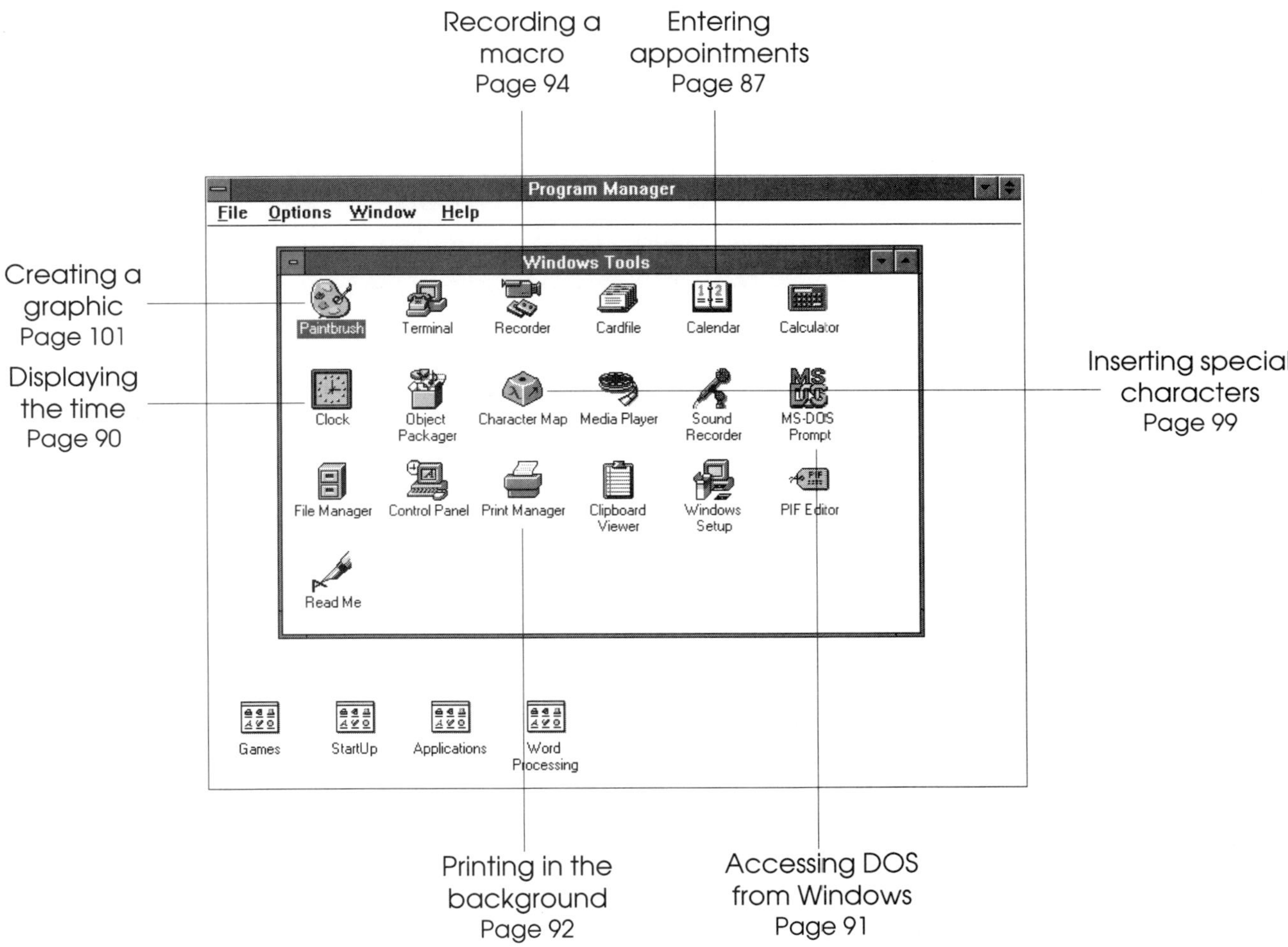

Recording a macro Page 94
Entering appointments Page 87
Creating a graphic Page 101
Displaying the time Page 90
Inserting special characters Page 99
Printing in the background Page 92
Accessing DOS from Windows Page 91
Program Manager
File Options Window Help
Windows Tools
Paintbrush
Terminal
Recorder
Cardfile
Calendar
Calculator
Clock
Object Packager
Character Map
Media Player
Sound Recorder
MS-DOS Prompt
File Manager
Control Panel
Print Manager
Clipboard Viewer
Windows Setup
PIF Editor
Read Me
Games
StartUp
Applications
Word Processing

Windows 3.1 comes with a grab bag of indispensable utilities and programs. If you've been following along with the examples in this book, all these tools are in the Windows Tools group in Program Manager, except for Notepad and Write, which are in the Word Processing group that you created in Chapter 2. If you haven't been following along, you'll find the tools distributed between the Main and Accessories group windows. To start any Windows tool, simply double-click its icon.

Some of the Windows tools are quite large and involved, and others are quite small and simple. You'll use some of them often and others rarely, if ever. We've already introduced two useful tools, Notepad and Calculator. We've also looked at Clipboard Viewer and File Manager. In this chapter, we first show you how to work with Cardfile and Calendar—electronic equivalents of a Rolodex and appointment book—and then we give you an overview of the other tools we think you'll use regularly, finishing with an example of what you can do with Write and Paintbrush. (We briefly discuss the remaining tools, which are primarily for display and system configuration, in Chapter 6.) Our goal is to tell you enough to get you going so that you can experiment on your own.

Cardfile

You use Cardfile to keep track of addresses and phone numbers, or any similar set of information, by recording the pertinent information on cards. Cardfile automatically alphabetizes the cards and, if you have a modem, can even dial the phone number on a card for you.

The people at CityRock Gym in Emeryville, California could use Cardfile to record the names and addresses of members. Here's how they might set up and use this handy tool:

Starting Cardfile

1. Start the Cardfile program by double-clicking its icon in Program Manager. Cardfile opens with one blank card displayed in its window. The card is divided into two areas: an index line (used for alphabetizing) at the top of the card, and an information area below it, like this:

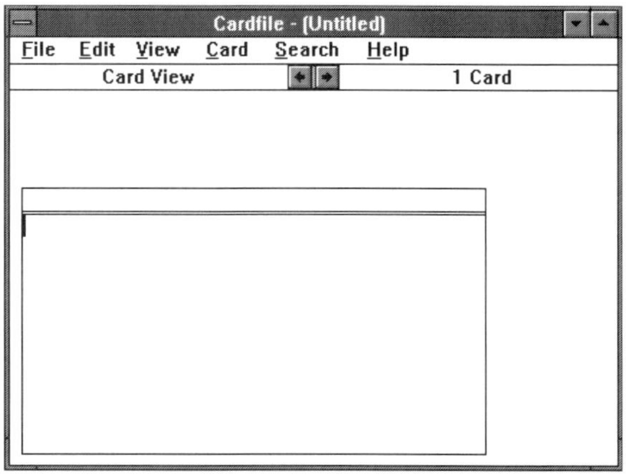

2. Choose Index from the Edit menu to display this dialog box:

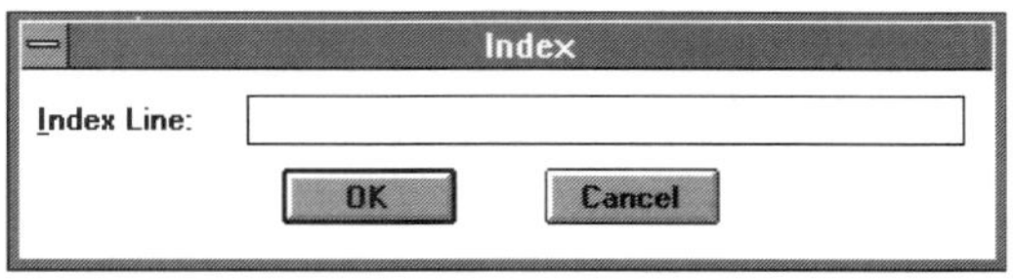

3. Type a name with the last name first (for example, *Miller, Jocelyn*), and click OK. Cardfile closes the dialog box, enters the name on the card's index line, and moves the insertion point to the information area.

4. Type the address and phone number shown here, pressing Enter when you need to start a new line:

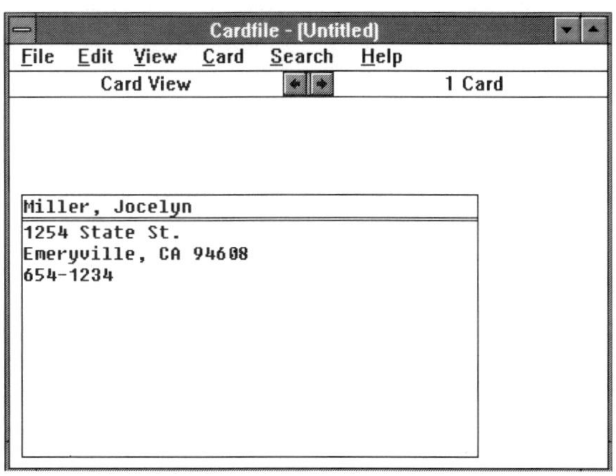

You can type up to 11 lines of text on a card, and you can paste in unformatted text from other applications, such as Notepad.

Adding cards

5. To add another card, choose Add from the Card menu. Cardfile displays the dialog box on the next page.

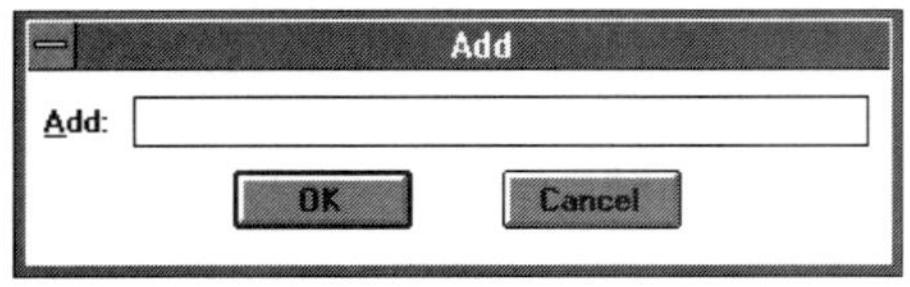

6. Type the name you want to appear on the index line of the new card, and click OK. Cardfile displays a new card on top of the first card, with the insertion point in the information area and the index line of the first card visible behind the new card.

Editing Cards

If you want to create a card that is similar to a card you have already created, you can copy the existing card and then edit it. For example, here's how the people at CityRock Gym would create a card for David Miller, Jocelyn's husband:

Duplicating cards

1. Click the card for Jocelyn Miller to bring it to the top of the stack, and choose Duplicate from the Card menu. An exact copy of the card appears in the window.
2. Double-click the index line, or choose Index from the Edit menu. Cardfile displays the Index dialog box.
3. Select the word *Jocelyn*, overwrite it by typing *David*, and click OK.
4. Edit the text in the information area as necessary.

If you edit a card and then want to return it to its previous state, before doing anything else—such as selecting another card—choose Restore from the Edit menu. Cardfile then undoes any changes you have made to the active card.

Deleting cards

To delete a card, bring the card you want to delete to the top of the stack, and choose Delete from the Card menu. A dialog box asks you to confirm the command. Click OK, and Cardfile deletes the card.

Displaying Cards

Below the menu bar, Cardfile indicates how many cards are in the stack. The arrows to the left of the number of cards let you flip back and forth through the cards one at a time. To jump quickly to another card in the stack, simply click the card's index line to bring that card to the front of the stack.

If you have a large stack of cards, as CityRock Gym would have, you might want to display just their index lines, instead of complete cards. To see only the index lines, choose List from the View menu. List View shows an alphabetized list of the index lines of all the cards in the stack. To move to a particular card in the stack, click the index line of the card you want, and then choose Card from the View menu. Cardfile switches back to Card View, with the selected card at the top of the stack.

List View

When you have accumulated a large number of cards, you can use menu commands to quickly display a specific card. For example, if the people at CityRock Gym want to display the address of a particular club member, they can choose Go To from the Search menu and enter the member's name in the Go To dialog box. (If they are uncertain about the spelling of the name, they can enter just a part of it. And they don't need to worry about capital letters, because Go To searches are not case sensitive.)

Suppose CityRock Gym wants to do a bulk mailing to all members in a certain ZIP code. To search the addresses in the information area, they can choose Find from the Search menu in Card View and enter in the Find dialog box the ZIP codes they want to search for. If Cardfile finds a match, it puts the matching card at the top of the stack and highlights the matching text. Clicking Find Next locates the next instance of the search text.

Saving, Printing, and Merging

You save a Cardfile file the same way you save any other Windows file. Simply use the Save or Save As command on the File menu. By default, Windows assigns a CRD extension to a Cardfile document.

You use the Print command on the File menu to print the card at the top of the stack in Card View, and you use Print All to print all the cards in the stack, with three cards to a page. The cards are printed just as they appear in Card View, with a

Dialing from Cardfile

If you have a modem, you can use Cardfile to dial the phone number recorded on a card. Select the card, highlight the number, and choose Autodial from the Card menu. In the Autodial dialog box, make any adjustments necessary for automatic dialing, such as adding a prefix, and click OK. When the phone rings, pick up your phone and wait for an answer.

border and an index line. See "Print Manager and Printing" on page 91 for more information about printing.

You can join two saved Cardfile files to create one file by using the Merge command on the File menu. For example, CityRock Gym might want to combine a file of members' names and addresses with a file of vendors' names and addresses to create a list of people to whom they want to send season's greetings at the end of the year. To merge two files, you open one Cardfile file, and choose Merge from the File menu. In the File Merge dialog box, you highlight the name of the file you want to merge into the open file, and click OK. The cards from the two files are combined and alphabetized, and the card-count indicator reflects the new number of cards. If you want to keep the merged file, save it with a name that is different from those of both of the files from which it was created.

Calendar

You can use Calendar to remind yourself of important events at work or at home. Its alarm feature can even give you advance notice of appointments.

Entering Appointments

At CityRock Gym, they might use Calendar to record appointments for prospective members to tour the facilities or to schedule special classes. Here's how to enter appointments:

Cardfile graphics

Any bitmap graphic created in a Windows paint program, such as Paintbrush, can be pasted onto a Cardfile card. (Before you choose Paste or Paste Special, you must choose Picture from Cardfile's Edit menu.) You can even combine text and graphics. The graphic can be any size; Cardfile scales it to fit in the information area of the card. Scaling doesn't affect the properties of the graphic, and you can later copy it from Cardfile and paste it into a graphics program, where it will appear in its original size.

Printing Rolodex cards

If you want to use a Cardfile address database in a desktop Rolodex, you can print the database file on special perforated card stock. Use the settings in the Page Setup dialog box to align the addresses so that they print within the margins of the cards.

Starting Calendar

1. Double-click the Calendar icon in Program Manager. This new, untitled Calendar window appears, with the current date and time at the top and an appointment area, divided into one-hour time intervals, below:

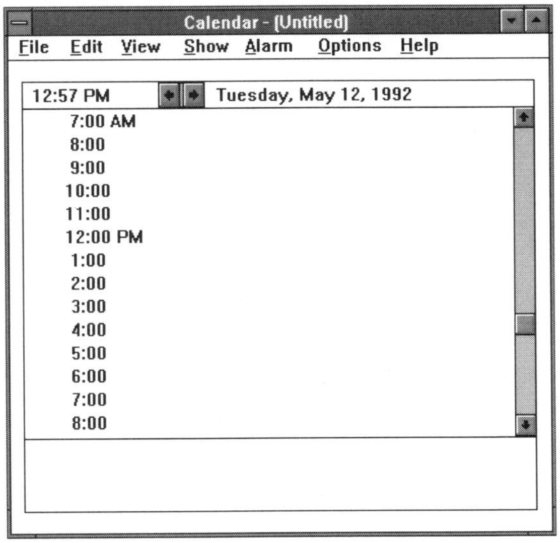

Entering appointments

2. To make an appointment for Barry Scott at 3:00 PM this afternoon, click to the right of that time in the appointment area, and type *Barry Scott.*
3. You can use the notes area below the appointment area for any general notes pertaining to this date. Type *Deadline for Climbing Magazine ad.*

Changing time intervals

You can change the one-hour time intervals to 15-minute or 30-minute intervals and the 12-hour format to 24-hour format, and you can change the 7:00 AM starting time. Simply choose Day Settings from the Options menu, and make the necessary changes. When you click OK, the appointment area will reflect your selections.

Suppose that Amanda Rawlings wants to tour CityRock Gym at 4:15 PM tomorrow. To display tomorrow's appointment area, follow these steps:

1. Click the right arrow at the top of the appointment area to move forward one day. The date above the appointment area changes to tomorrow's date.

Inserting non-standard times

2. To insert a special time slot in the appointment area without changing the one-hour format of the entire file, choose Special Time from the Options menu to display this dialog box:

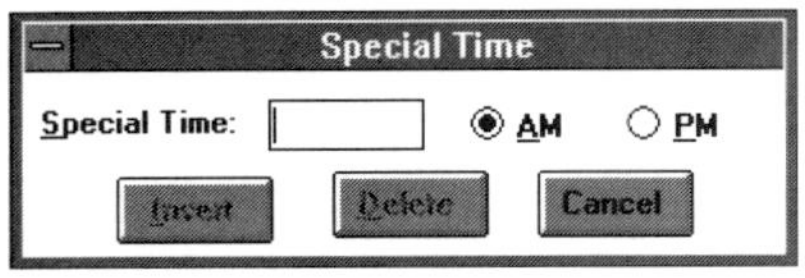

3. Type 4:15 in the Special Time text box, and click the PM button. Finally, click Insert. Calendar closes the dialog box and adds the new time slot to the appointment area, like this:

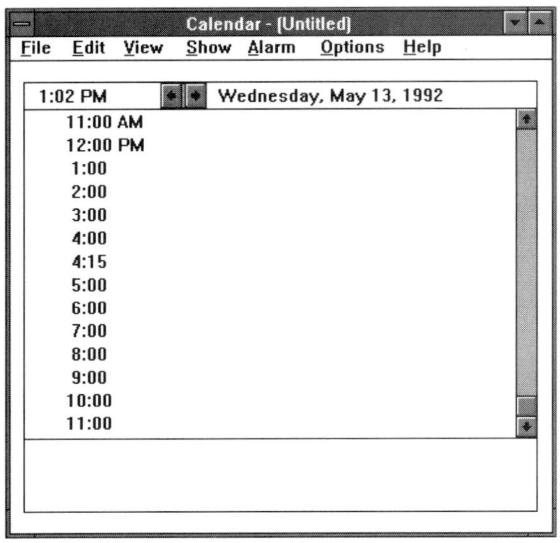

4. Enter the appointment for Amanda Rawlings.

5. Click the left arrow at the top of the appointment area to move back to the calendar for today.

If Amanda Rawlings cancels her appointment and you need to delete the special time slot, you simply click an insertion point in the time slot, choose Special Time from the Options menu, and click Delete.

Displaying Days and Months

Calendar allows you to display different days in a variety of ways. As you've seen, one way of navigating through a Calendar file is to click the left and right scroll arrows at the top of the appointment area. You can also use the commands on the Show menu. Choosing Today displays the current day, choosing Previous takes you back one day in the calendar, and choosing Next takes you forward one day. Use the Date command to move quickly to a specific date.

Month View

You can display Calendar in Month View rather than Day View, either by choosing Month from the View menu or by double-clicking the date above the appointment area. The whole month is then displayed, with the date that was active in Day View highlighted. The scroll arrows above the appointment area and the commands on the Show menu now move you through the Calendar file in months instead of days.

Setting Alarms

You can set alarms to remind you of important appointments, by using the commands on the Alarm menu. If you use alarms, you should always work with Calendar running in the background; otherwise, the alarms can't sound.

To set an alarm, click an insertion point in the time slot at which you want the alarm to sound, and then choose Set from the Alarm menu. A small bell to the left of the time slot indicates that the alarm is set. When the time on your computer matches the alarm time, your computer beeps. If Calendar is running in the foreground, a dialog box displays any message you typed in the appointment area. If Calendar is running in a window in the background, the window's title bar flashes; if it is running as an icon, the icon flashes. Click the window or the icon to display the message.

You can use the Controls command on the Alarm menu to make all alarms go off from 1 to 10 minutes before the actual appointment time and to turn the alarm beep on and off.

Saving and Printing

Saving a Calendar file is similar to saving any Windows file. Just use the Save or Save As command on the File menu. Calendar adds a CAL extension to saved files.

You can use the Print command to print the information that appears in the appointment and notes areas. Simply choose Print from the File menu, and specify in the From and To boxes the days with the schedules you want to print. When printing, Calendar skips over days and time slots that have no entries.

Clock

The simplest of the Windows tools, Clock has just one function: to tell the time in either analog or digital format. Double-clicking the Clock icon displays a small window with a clock face on it. Use the Settings menu to switch between the analog and digital clock face, set the digital clock font, remove the title bar from the clock window (simply double-click anywhere on the clock face to display the title bar again), and toggle the date and seconds on and off. You can resize Clock to be full screen, or shrink it down to an icon. The minimized Clock icon then displays the current time and date.

If you want the clock to be displayed at all times, use the following settings:

Displaying the time

1. Double-click the Clock icon in the Windows Tools window, and then choose Analog or Digital from the Settings menu, depending on which clock face you prefer.
2. Be sure the No Title, Seconds, and Date commands on the Settings menu are turned off (no check mark is beside them).
3. Then make the clock very small, and move it to an out-of-the-way spot, such as the title bar of a maximized window.
4. Next choose Always On Top from Clock's Control menu to have the time appear to float above all other applications.
5. Finally, switch to Program Manager, and copy Clock's icon (hold down Ctrl while you drag the icon) into the StartUp group window so that Windows will start Clock automatically every time you start Windows.

Resetting the time

The time displayed by Clock reflects your system time, which is either set by you each time you boot your computer or held in memory by a battery. You can change the time using either MS-DOS Prompt or Control Panel.

MS-DOS Prompt

MS-DOS Prompt duplicates the DOS command interface. You can use it to type DOS commands, just as you would on the DOS command line, without leaving Windows. For example, you might use MS-DOS Prompt to run a non-Windows utility, such as an archiving program that requires you to type many parameters on the command line to specify precisely the type of archiving you want.

To use MS-DOS Prompt, double-click its icon in Program Manager. The DOS prompt appears, looking as though you have left Windows and returned to DOS. But rest assured: You are still in Windows. Type the DOS command, just as you usually would. The command should function normally. When it finishes, the DOS prompt is redisplayed. To return to Windows, type *exit*, and press Enter.

Print Manager and Printing

When you ran Setup to install Windows for the first time, you probably indicated the type of printer or printers you intended to use. After installing the printers, you follow the same basic procedure to print from all Windows tools and applications. The dialog boxes we discuss in this section are specific to your printer and the application you are printing from, but all share the same basic elements.

1. Choose Print Setup from the tool's or application's File menu.

MS-DOS Prompt no-no's

It's unwise to use utilities such as disk-defragmentation or file-unerase programs from MS-DOS Prompt, because they can change the locations of files that Windows needs to operate properly. Always exit Windows to run these types of programs.

DOS in a window

If you enter commands using MS-DOS Prompt often, and you run Windows in 386 Enhanced mode, you can run the DOS command line in a window. Just double-click the MS-DOS Prompt icon to get to the command line, and press Alt+Enter. The command line is displayed in a window. You can't close the window from the Control menu however, you must type *exit* at the command line.

2. In the Print Setup dialog box, select the printer you want.
3. If you need to configure the printer for a particular print job, click the Options or Setup button, make the necessary changes in the dialog box that appears, and then click OK.
4. Choose Page Setup from the File menu. In the Page Setup dialog box, you can set margins and create a header and a footer for your file, using these codes:

Creating headers and footers

Code	Function
&d	Inserts today's date.
&t	Inserts the current time.
&f	Inserts the current filename.
&p	Inserts the page number.
&l	Left aligns the header or footer.
&r	Right aligns the header or footer.
&c	Centers the header or footer.

You can combine these codes to make custom headers and footers. For example, to print a footer like this one at the bottom of the pages of a Notepad file:

Meeting Notes 5/12/92 Page 1

enter the following in the Footer text box:

&lMeeting Notes&c&d&rPage &p

5. When you have set up your pages, click OK.
6. Choose Print from the File menu. In the Print dialog box, you can often set more options, such as how many copies and what pages to print.
7. After completing this dialog box, click OK to begin printing.

The file is either sent directly to the printer or is sent to Print Manager, which then sends it to the printer. If you are not using Print Manager, you must wait for the file to finish printing before resuming your work.

Printing in the background

Print Manager, Windows' built-in print spooler, sends the file to the printer in the background while you carry out another task in the foreground. When you choose the Print command, Print Manager runs as a minimized icon and then closes itself when it has sent the last file in its list, or queue, to the printer.

Changing the print queue

If you are in the middle of printing several files and need to view or change the print queue, double-click the Print Manager icon or press Alt+Tab to bring Print Manager to the foreground. The Print Manager window appears with a list of the printers you are connected to and the files in the queue. The file that is currently printing has a small printer icon next to it, and other files have a number to the left of their names, indicating their position in the queue. You can change the order of files in the queue, remove files, and temporarily halt and then resume printing, all with a few mouse clicks. To have files print in a different order than the one specified by the queue, click a filename, and drag it to a new position. To delete a file from the queue, click its name, and then click the Delete button. To pause or resume a print job, click the printer's name, and then click Pause or Resume.

Recorder

The Recorder is a simple program that records a sequence—called a macro—of commands, actions, and characters that you enter using the keyboard or the mouse. You can then reproduce the sequence by pressing a shortcut key. You can save the macros you create in a Recorder file for future use. You can record many macros in a single Recorder file, and you can even merge Recorder files using the Merge command on the File menu.

Print Manager priority

The Low Priority, Medium Priority, and High Priority commands on the Print Manager Options menu dictate how fast files are printed and the extent to which Print Manager slows down the operation of foreground applications. Medium Priority is the default. Low Priority causes Print Manager to print more slowly but allocates more memory to foreground applications. If your foreground application runs too slowly while you are printing, try choosing Low Priority. If you have a very fast computer and the foreground application doesn't seem to be unduly affected by Print Manager, try choosing High Priority to speed up background printing.

Printing on a network

If you are on a network, you may want to turn Print Manager off, because most networks have built-in print spoolers. Leave it on if you want to be able to view the names of files you have sent to the printer.

Recorder is best suited for simple repetitive tasks, such as typing the closing of a letter in a word-processing program or formatting selected cells in a spreadsheet program. As a simple example, suppose Peter Mayfield of CityRock Gym frequently needs to list the names of his employees in various Notepad documents and he wants to be able to reproduce the list by pressing a few keys instead of typing it each time. Follow along as we record the list as a macro:

1. Start Notepad, the application in which you want to use the macro. Normally, you need to set up the document to the point where you can begin the sequence of steps you want to be able to reproduce. In this case, no setup is necessary.
2. Choose Switch To from the Control menu, select Program Manager, and then click the Switch To button.

Recording a macro

3. Start Recorder by double-clicking its icon, and then minimize Program Manager so that only the Notepad and Recorder windows are visible on your screen.
4. In the Recorder window, choose Record from the Macro menu to display the Record Macro dialog box:

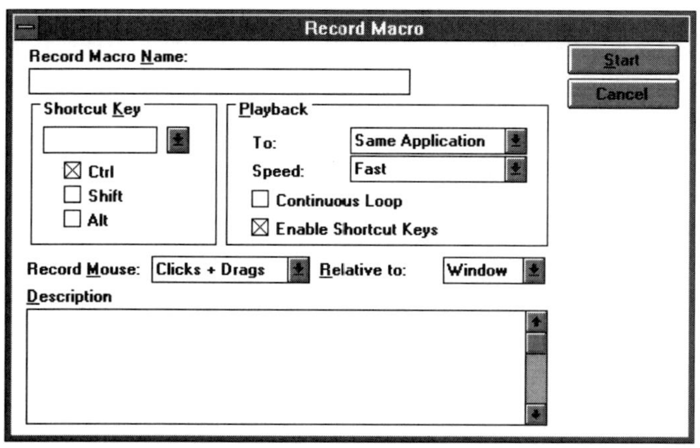

In this dialog box, you can set various options that tell Recorder how to record the macro and how to play it back when you use it later.

5. Type *emp_list* as the macro's name and *Employee List* as its description. In the Shortcut Key section, be sure Ctrl is selected, and then type *e* in the text box to designate Ctrl+E as your shortcut key combination. Select how mouse actions

will be recorded, and select the various Playback options. (You might need to experiment with different settings before your macro will record and run correctly.)

6. Click the Start button to begin the macro recording session. Recorder minimizes to a blinking icon, indicating that it is recording.
7. In the Notepad window (the window of the program in which you want to record the macro), type the following names on separate lines: *Hanneli*, *Amy*, *David*, *Bill*, *Mike*, and *Robin*.
8. When you're finished, click the blinking Recorder icon, which displays this dialog box:

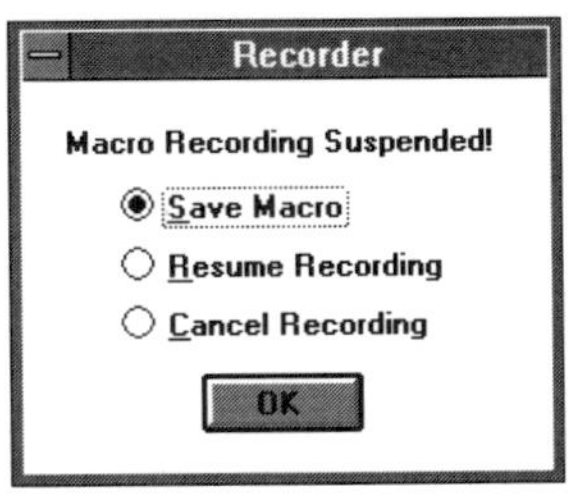

Here, you can either save the macro, resume recording, or cancel recording.

Saving a macro

9. Choose Save, and then double-click the Recorder icon. In the Recorder window, choose Save As from the File menu, type *emp* as the macro name, and click OK to preserve the macro

Recording mouse actions

Macro programs are notoriously unreliable when it comes to recording complex, exacting mouse movements. For example, you can't record a Paintbrush session and then expect Recorder (or any other macro program) to recreate your masterpiece. Whenever possible, use the keyboard equivalent for any mouse action.

Macros can't be edited

Think through the macro ahead of time. Any mistakes you make will be recorded. You can change many of the settings you made in the Record Macro dialog box, such as the macro's name, shortcut key, playback options, and description, by selecting the macro's name from the Recorder window and choosing Properties from the Macro menu. But you can't modify the macro itself.

Nested macros

You can nest macros up to five layers deep by pressing a macro's shortcut key while recording another macro. All the macros must be in the same open file for nesting to work.

for future use. Recorder automatically appends the REC extension to the name.

To run the macro in the future:

Running a macro

1. Double-click the Recorder icon to open the Recorder window, choose the Open command from the File menu, and double-click the EMP.REC filename.
2. Switch to Program Manager, and open a new Notepad document window.
3. Press Ctrl+E, the assigned shortcut key. (You can also run the macro by selecting it in the Recorder window or by choosing the Run command from the Macro menu.) Recorder minimizes to an icon and plays back the macro. The new document now lists the five CityRock employees.

Canceling a macro

You can cancel a macro in progress by pressing Ctrl+Break.

To change the settings you made for the macro in the Record Macro dialog box, highlight the macro's name in the Recorder window, and choose Properties from the Macro menu. In the Macro Properties dialog box, you can change the macro's name, shortcut key, playback options, and description.

Object Packager

You use Object Packager to create a package consisting of an icon and a document (or part of one). The icon represents the document. You can then copy the icon/document package and insert it in another document that supports object linking and embedding (OLE). Opening the package displays the linked or embedded object.

Clicking the Object Packager icon displays this window:

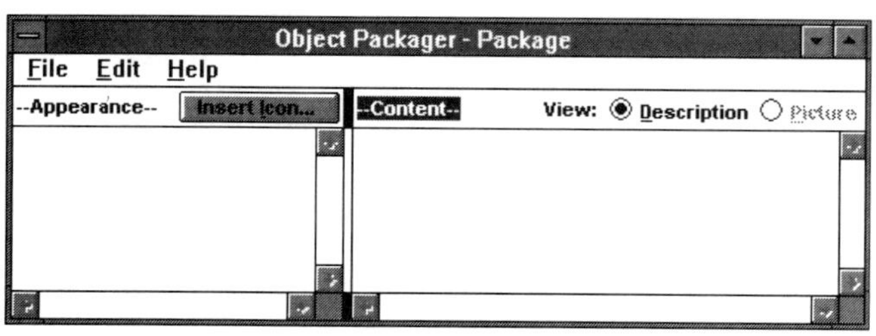

As an example, suppose you import one of the bitmap files that comes with Windows (those with BMP extensions) into Object Packager. The program automatically assigns the bitmap file the Paintbrush icon. You can then use the Copy Package command on the Edit menu to copy the icon, switch to Write (or any application that supports linking or embedding), choose the Paste Special command, and specify that you want to embed a Package Object. The Paintbrush icon then appears in the Write document. Double-clicking the icon automatically starts Paintbrush and displays the bitmap graphic. You might also want to create a sound object package and embed its icon—which looks like a microphone—in a document. Double-clicking the microphone icon in the document would then start Sound Recorder (discussed on the next page) and play the sound (provided, of course, that you have a sound card).

Inserting an object package

A quick way to insert an object package in a document is to use File Manager. Set up the document window and the File Manager window so that you can see both the object icon's name (such as CASTLE.BMP) and the document, and then drag the object icon's name to the document. An Object Package icon automatically appears, and you can then double-click the icon to see or hear the object.

Object Linking and Embedding (OLE)

Some Windows applications support object linking and embedding, or OLE. OLE goes several steps beyond simple cutting and pasting to create a conduit between a source and a destination document. Both source and destination applications must support OLE. Although the terms *linking* and *embedding* are lumped together, they are quite different. Linking allows some programs to automatically update pasted data. For example, you can paste an Excel worksheet into a Word for Windows document in such a way that, whenever you change the worksheet data, the Word document is updated correspondingly. Embedding is used to paste an object that doesn't necessarily need to be updated, but may need to be changed by the originating program. For example, if you embed a Paintbrush graphic in a Write document and need to change some aspect of the graphic, you can double-click the embedded bitmap image to open a window to Paintbrush within Write and make the changes. You must have enough memory to run both programs at the same time. Commands for linking and embedding are not identical in all programs that support it, but they always appear in the Edit menu as some variation of Paste Special or Insert Object.

Media Player

Media Player allows you to control devices such as CD-ROM drives and videodisc players so that you can run animation, sound, and MIDI (musical instrument digital interface) files. When you click the Media Player icon, you see this window:

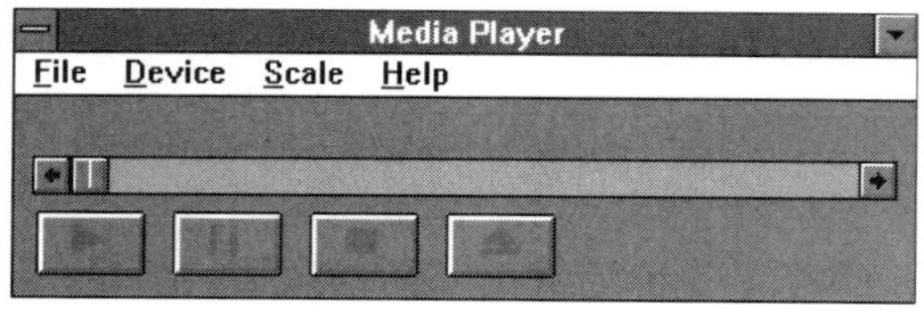

Devices are either simple or compound. An example of a simple device is an audio CD player that plays only the CD it currently holds. An example of a complex device is a sound card for which you must specify the file to be played. Once you have selected the device and media file, you use the buttons in the Media Player window to play the file.

For Windows to recognize a media hardware device, you must install the correct device driver using the Control Panel Drivers option (see page 116 for more information).

Sound Recorder

If you have recording and playback devices attached to your computer and have installed the appropriate device drivers, Sound Recorder enables you to record, edit, and play sound files. Clicking the Sound Recorder icon displays this window:

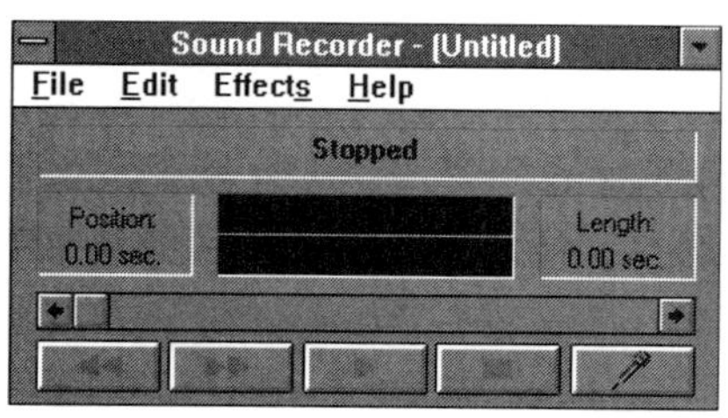

You use Sound Recorder's File menu to open and save sound files, and you use the buttons in the Sound Recorder window just like the rewind, fast forward, play, pause, and record buttons on a cassette player. You can have fun being a junior recording-studio engineer by choosing the Edit and Effects menu commands to merge, speed up, and reverse sounds.

Character Map

You use Character Map to track down elusive characters and symbols that you want to insert in your documents. Suppose you're in the middle of a document and you need to insert a registered trademark symbol. Simply double-click the Character Map icon to display this window:

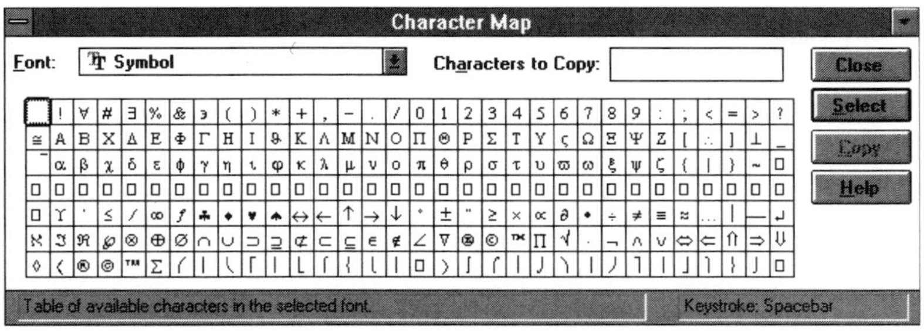

Finding a character

Select a font from the Font drop-down list (be sure the font is also available in the application you're using). Then locate the character you need. Click a character to see an enlargement of it. Add the character to the Characters To Copy text box by double-clicking it, or by selecting it and clicking Select. Then you can click Copy, switch back to your document, and simply paste in the character.

Terminal

Terminal is a full-featured telecommunications program that allows you to connect your computer via modem to online services, bulletin boards, and other computers. After you have connected your modem, double-click the Terminal icon to display this window:

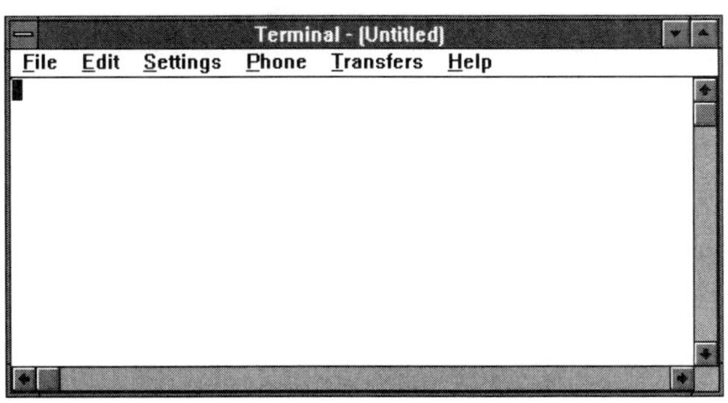

Use the commands on the Settings menu to choose terminal, transfer, communications, and modem settings. Then use the Dial command on the Phone menu to dial phone numbers, and use the commands on the Transfers menu to upload (send) and download (receive) files.

To transfer a file while working in another program, make Terminal active, begin the transfer, minimize Terminal to an icon, and then switch to the other program. When the transfer is complete, the computer beeps, and the Terminal icon flashes. Simply activate Terminal to finish the online session.

Communications macros

If you use Terminal often, you will want to create macros so that you can carry out common procedures by clicking buttons at the bottom of the Terminal window. Choose Function Keys from the Settings menu to display this dialog box:

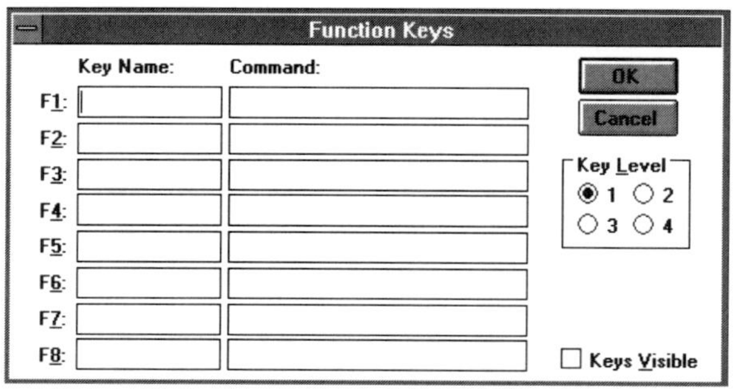

You can create up to eight macros in this dialog box. If you fill up all the slots, you can select another level to display eight

Dialing macros

If you get tired of using the Phone Number dialog box each time you want to dial a different number, create a set of macros to dial numbers you use often. Preface the number with all the necessary modem commands. For example, you could create the following macro to dial a number on a Hayes-compatible modem hooked up to a touch-tone phone system:

ATDT5551212^M.

Remember to include a carriage return to send the command.

Turn on Local Echo in the Terminal Preferences dialog box to see the command displayed on the screen.

You can enter up to 41 characters for the macro sequence. Use the Recorder tool to create longer, more complex macros.

Macro buttons

Select the Keys Visible option in the Function Keys dialog box to display the macros you define as buttons at the bottom of the Terminal window. To cycle through the four levels of macros, click the Level button in the bottom-right corner. To use a macro, click its button.

more slots. A total of four macro levels allows you to create up to 32 macros. You use these control codes to write macros:

Code	Function
^A–^Z	Sends control codes A through Z to the remote computer. Common control codes are ^H (backspace), ^J (line feed), and ^M (carriage return).
^$D<##>	Pauses for ## seconds before continuing the macro.
^$B	Sends a break code.
^$C	Dials the phone number you entered using the Dial command.
^$H	Hangs up the phone.
^$L1–^$L4	Changes to another macro level.

For example, this macro logs on to the GEnie online service:

^$C^$D03HHH^M^$D02xth4209,antwerp^M

The macro dials a predefined number, pauses for 3 seconds, types a 3-letter logon code and a carriage return, pauses for 2 seconds, and then types a password and a carriage return. Using combinations of control codes, you can write some pretty slick macros, but usually Terminal macros perform simple, repetitive tasks, such as logging on or off a service. Remember to give each macro a descriptive name and to save the Terminal file so that you can use the macros in the future.

Write and Paintbrush

In this section, we'll give you a taste of the Windows Write and Paintbrush applications by showing how you might use them to create a document. Our intent here is not to give you detailed instructions, but to give you an idea of what you can do with these applications. If you are familiar with word-processing and paint programs, you'll soon figure out these Windows applications by playing around with them.

Creating a graphic

For our example document, we've recreated a version of the Grand Opening announcement for CityRock Gym. The finished piece is a letter-sized flyer. To create the announcement, we first double-clicked the Paintbrush icon in Program

Manager to open the Windows paint program. Using the Curve tool (which draws arcs), the Line tool, the Paint Roller, and the Text tool, we created CityRock's logo, a stylized climber. We then used the Line and Text tools to create a map giving directions to the club, like this:

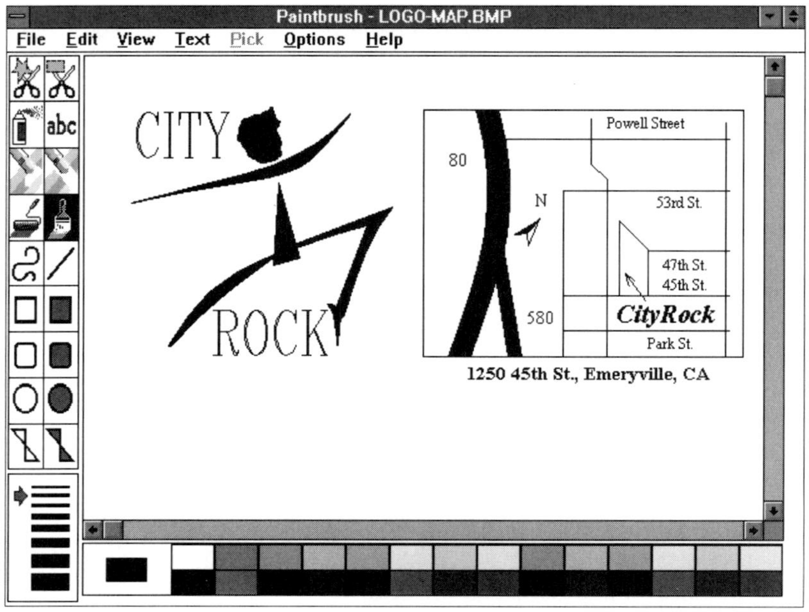

We placed the two graphics side by side and, after selecting them both with the Pick tool (cropping as closely as possible), we copied them to the Clipboard. We chose Save As from the File menu and saved the graphics with the filename LOGO-MAP. Because we didn't specify a directory and filename extension, the graphic document was saved in the WINDOWS directory and was given the extension BMP to indicate that the file was created in the Paintbrush program. Then we chose Exit from the File menu to quit Paintbrush.

Embedding a graphic

In Program Manager, we started Write by double-clicking its icon. We immediately chose Paste Special from the Edit menu to embed a copy of the Paintbrush object at the top of the blank document window. We could have chosen Paste, but embedding the object makes it easier to edit it in the future. We then chose Move Picture from the Edit menu to center the graphic. We keyed in the text of the announcement, without worrying about formatting, and then started experimenting. We set margins, indents, and tabs by moving icons on the ruler at the top of the Write window, and we chose different fonts, sizes, and styles from the Character menu, until we were satisfied with the results, which are shown here:

Formatting text

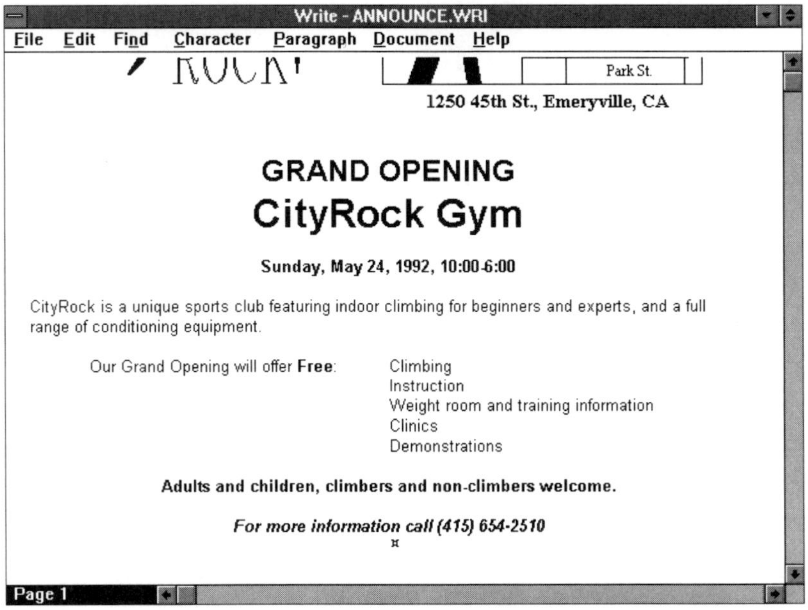

Next, we chose Save As from the File menu and saved the document with the name ANNOUNCE. The file was automatically given the extension WRI to indicate that we created the document in Write. Finally, we printed the document by choosing Print from the File menu.

6

The System Configuration Tools

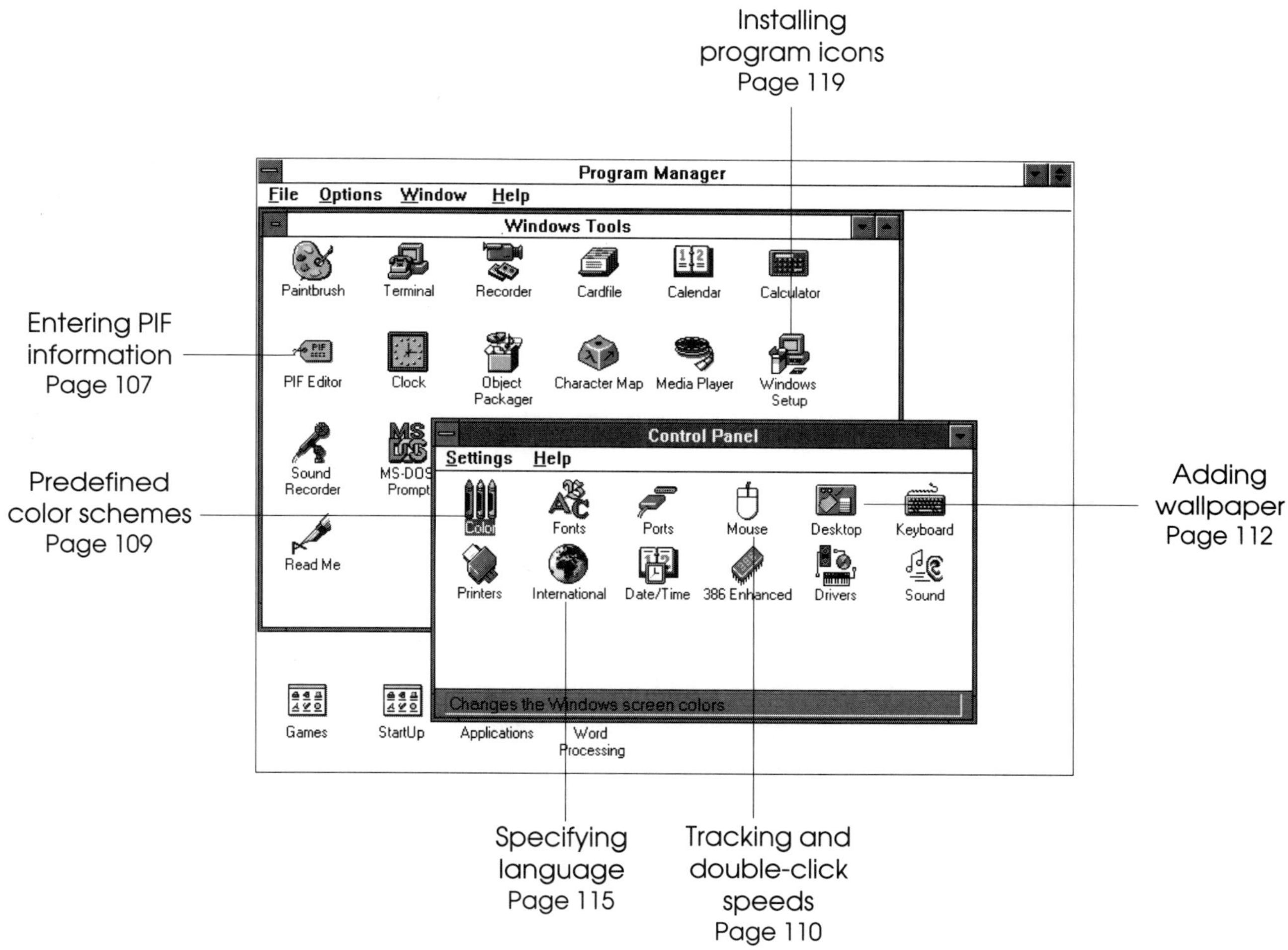
Installing program icons Page 119
Entering PIF information Page 107
Predefined color schemes Page 109
Adding wallpaper Page 112
Specifying language Page 115
Tracking and double-click speeds Page 110
Program Manager
File Options Window Help
Windows Tools
Paintbrush
Terminal
Recorder
Cardfile
Calendar
Calculator
PIF Editor
Clock
Object Packager
Character Map
Media Player
Windows Setup
Sound Recorder
Read Me
Control Panel
Settings Help
Color
Fonts
Ports
Mouse
Desktop
Keyboard
Printers
International
Date/Time
386 Enhanced
Drivers
Sound
Changes the Windows screen colors
Games
StartUp
Applications
Word Processing

In this chapter, we give you a brief overview of the Windows 3.1 tools that allow you to configure your system. We've grouped these programs in this last chapter because we feel you are less likely to use them when you first start using Windows 3.1 than the tools presented in Chapter 5. If you've been following along with the examples in this book, these tools are in the Windows Tools group in Program Manager, together with many of the tools discussed in the previous chapter. If you haven't been following along, you'll find the tools in either the Main or Accessories group windows.

PIF Editor

When you ran the Windows Setup program, Windows created a Program Information File (PIF) for the non-Windows applications it recognized among the programs stored on your hard drive. Each PIF is a small settings file that helps Windows load the corresponding application, by designating where the program is located and how much memory it requires.

If Windows didn't recognize one of your applications when you ran Windows Setup, it will use a generic, default PIF for the application. If the application doesn't run properly, you need to use PIF Editor to write a PIF so that you can run the application from within Windows. It's not as hard as it sounds. Start by double-clicking the PIF Editor icon to open the PIF Editor window, which looks like this:

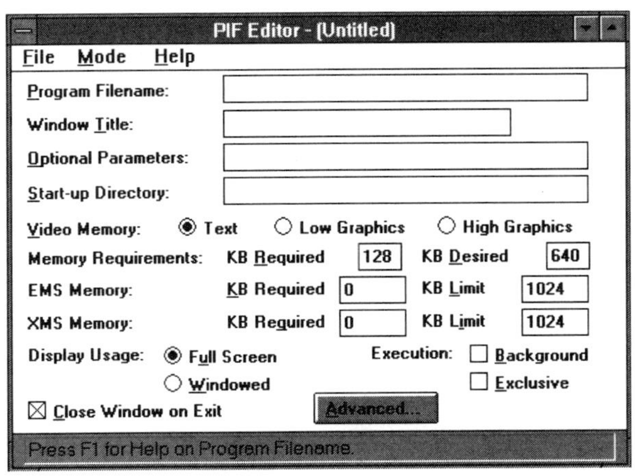

Entering PIF information

As you can see, this dialog box gives you a structured way of entering information about the application, as follows:

- In the Program Filename text box, type the path and filename of the non-Windows application.
- In the Window Title text box, type the name you want for the application's icon in Program Manager.
- In the Optional Parameters text box, type any parameters you would normally enter to run the application from the DOS prompt. (You can leave this box blank.)
- In the Start-Up Directory text box, type the name of the application's "working" directory—the place where you want to save and retrieve documents.
- If you are running Windows in 386 Enhanced mode and you want to run the application in a window, select the Windowed option.

Don't worry about the other options in the PIF Editor window for now. Simply choose Save As from the File menu and, in the Save As dialog box, type the name of the program, and click OK. PIF Editor adds a PIF extension and saves the file in the WINDOWS directory.

The next step is to link the PIF to the application's icon. Follow the process described on page 35 for creating a document icon, and enter the PIF name in the Command Line text box in the Program Item Properties dialog box.

After you create the icon, you can double-click it in Program Manager to start the application. Depending on which mode Windows is running in, the application might look a bit different than usual. If it crashes or misbehaves in any way, you can try adjusting the PIF to correct the problem. Start PIF Editor again, and open the PIF for the application so that you can change the settings. (If you need more information about setting specific options in the PIF Editor window, consult Windows Help or check the documentation.)

Quick start for programs

As far as Windows is concerned, a PIF file is the same as any other executable file. You can create an icon for a PIF file in Program Manager and double-click it to start the program it is linked to.

Control Panel

Control Panel controls how Windows runs and looks on your computer. A window something like this one is displayed when you double-click the Control Panel icon in Program Manager:

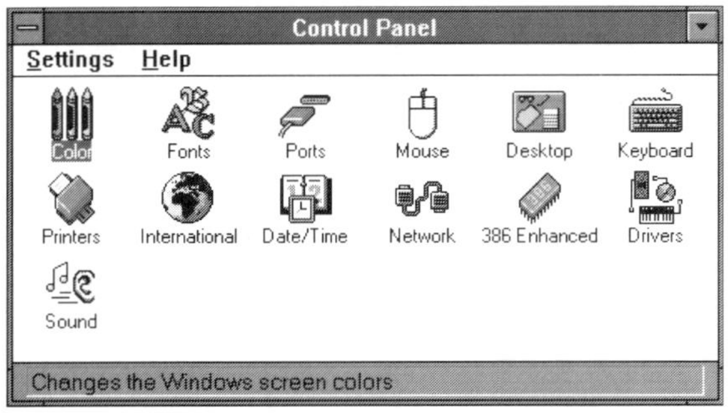

The icons in the window function like program icons, but they can't be moved, copied, or deleted. Your Control Panel window might not have all these icons, and it will have an additional icon if you are using Windows on a network. Let's look briefly at each of these options.

Color

You use the Color option to set the colors of many of Windows' standard elements, such as the scroll bars and the active title bar. Double-clicking Color displays this dialog box:

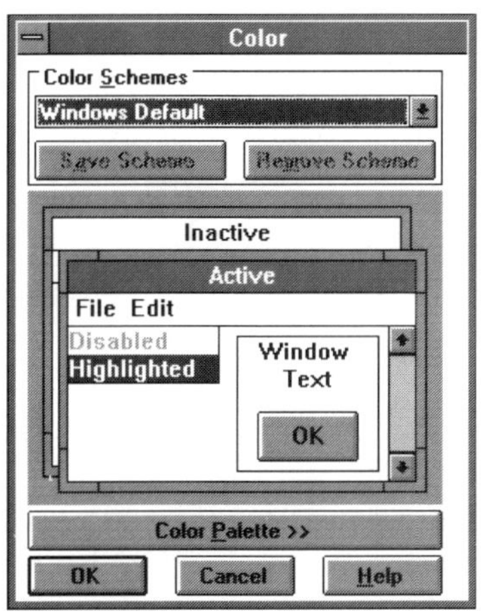

Predefined color schemes

You can select a preset color scheme, such as Tweed or Bordeaux, or you can design one of your own. When you select a new color scheme and click OK, your color changes are immediately reflected on the Windows screen.

Playing with colors can be fun, and we encourage you to experiment with this feature to learn more about it. We also recommend that you choose colors that are easy on the eyes, especially if you use Windows a lot. If you get tired of looking at a particular color combination (just try looking at Hotdog Stand for more than 5 minutes), you can select the Windows Default color scheme to revert to the original colors.

Fonts

With the Fonts option, you can add screen, plotter, and TrueType fonts for use with applications such as Write and Paintbrush. You can also use Fonts to remove a font. When you installed Windows, the Windows Setup program installed several fonts, each of which uses a small amount of memory and disk space. If you think you won't use a particular font, you can use this Fonts dialog box to remove it:

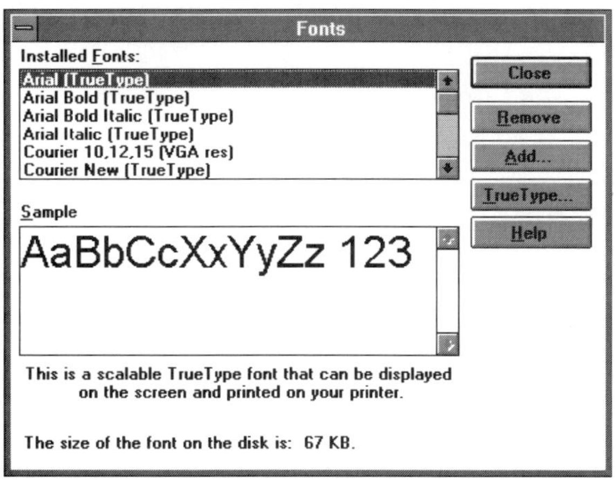

By default, Windows simply removes the font from memory; Windows also removes the font from your hard disk if you tell it to do so. One font you don't want to remove is MS Sans Serif, which Windows uses for the text in most of its dialog boxes.

TrueType

TrueType fonts are scaleable fonts. They appear exactly on the screen as they will print. These fonts appear with a TT symbol next to them in application font lists to indicate they are TrueType fonts. If you experiment with these fonts, you will see that they appear quite crisp on the screen, no matter what font size you choose. If you obtain additional TrueType fonts, you can add them using the Fonts dialog box.

Ports

Double-clicking Ports displays this dialog box, in which you configure the communications setting for your serial ports:

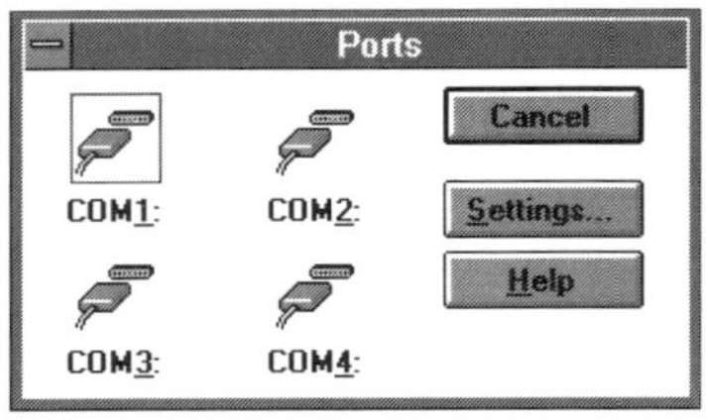

The serial ports are used by external devices such as printers and modems. Select the port icon for the port you want to configure, and click Settings. In the Settings dialog box, you can set the port's baud rate, parity, flow control, and data and stop bits. Advanced settings allow you to set the base I/O address and interrupt request line (IRQ). See your modem or printer documentation for device-specific settings.

Mouse

Double-clicking the Mouse icon displays this dialog box, in which you can set your mouse tracking speed and double-click speed:

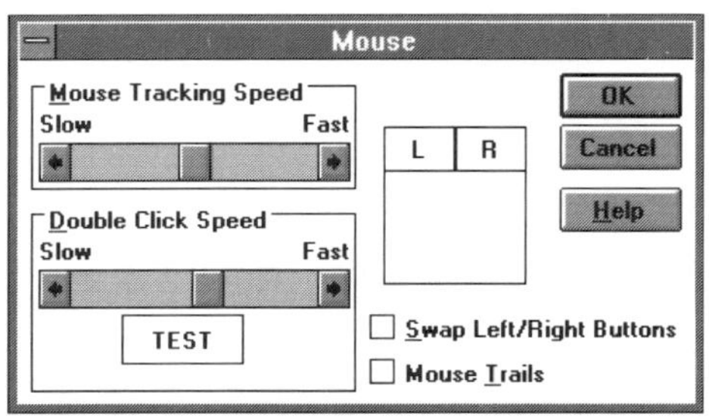

You can also use this option to switch the function of the left and right buttons and to set up the mouse for use with an LCD screen.

Tracking and double-click speeds

For both tracking speed and double-click speed, you select a speed from Slow to Fast on a scroll bar. Tracking speed is the distance the pointer moves compared with the distance the mouse moves. A fast tracking speed means the pointer moves a long way on the screen when you move the mouse a comparatively short distance on your desk. Double-click speed is the rate at which you must double-click an icon or a list item to activate it. A fast double-click speed means you must double-click very quickly. Unless you drink a lot of coffee, it's probably best not to set the double-click speed at its fastest setting. Use the TEST button below the Double Click Speed scroll bar to try out a new double-click speed. The button toggles from white to black or from black to white when you double-click it at the correct speed.

Swapping buttons

The Swap Left/Right Buttons option does just what it says. If you are a southpaw and find it easier to click and highlight text with the right mouse button instead of the left, select this option. The switch takes place immediately; you'll need to use the right mouse button to click OK to close the dialog box.

Mouse visibility on LCD screens

The Mouse Trails option can help improve the visibilty of the mouse pointer on LCD screens by creating a "trail" as the pointer moves across the screen. This option also takes effect immediately. It is also fun to play with for a minute or two, even on regular screens.

Desktop

The desktop is the surface behind all windows, window icons, and minimized program icons. Think of it as the screen that Windows uses to block out the DOS prompt. Double-clicking the Desktop icon displays this dialog box, in which you can change the default solid pattern of the desktop, use a bitmap graphic as desktop "wallpaper," set icon and window spacing, enable fast task switching, set the cursor blink rate, and enable a simple screen saver:

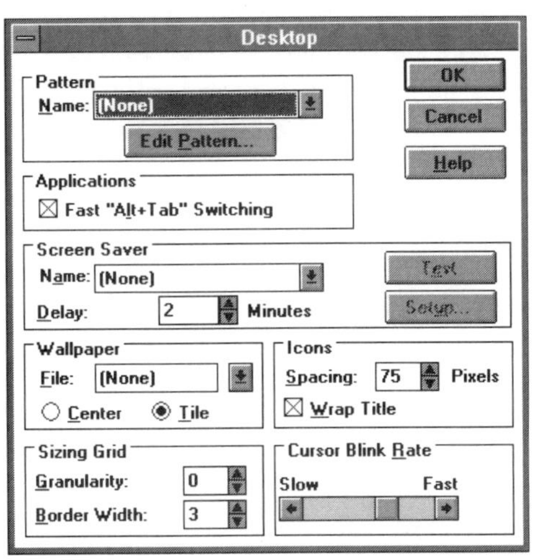

Changing patterns

To change the desktop pattern, select the pattern you want from the Name drop-down list. (You cannot see the desktop pattern or wallpaper if Program Manager is maximized.) Click the Edit Pattern button to bring up a dialog box in which you can edit the pattern, create your own pattern, and remove patterns from the list.

Adding wallpaper

In addition to using a background pattern, you can also use any bitmap graphic file in the WINDOWS directory as wallpaper. The default wallpaper is None. You can use the bitmap images that come with Windows for wallpaper, or you can create your own using Paintbrush. Select the wallpaper graphic file from the File drop-down list, and then select Center to place the graphic in the middle of the desktop or Tile to fill the entire desktop with tiled copies of the graphic. (Using Tile or using a very large graphic obscures any desktop pattern you have chosen.) Large and colorful wallpaper files can really eat up memory, so if you're low on memory, you might want to skip the wallpaper.

Setting distance between icons

The Spacing setting lets you set the distance that appears between icons when you choose the Arrange Icons command. Normally, the spacing set by Windows is adequate, but if you want more or less space between icons, use this option to change the setting.

Wrapping icon titles

The Wrap Title option, which is turned on by default, wraps icon titles that are very long.

Settings for windows

The Sizing Grid settings, Granularity and Border Width, determine how windows are placed on the desktop and how window borders appear. The Granularity setting creates an invisible grid with which windows and icons align. The default Granularity setting is 0, or no grid. Making this setting greater than 0 can help keep your desktop neat, but also prevents you from placing an icon anywhere that doesn't align with the grid. The Border Width setting determines the width of window borders. The default width is 3. If you find this border too thin to easily grab when resizing windows, you can make the Border Width setting larger.

Alt+Tab switching

By default, the Fast "Alt+Tab" Switching option in the Desktop dialog box is turned on so that you can quickly switch between open programs by pressing Alt+Tab. (We discussed Alt+Tab switching on page 67.)

Cursor blink rate

The Cursor Blink Rate sets the speed at which the insertion point blinks in any Windows program or dialog box that uses text. If the insertion point doesn't blink fast enough to catch your attention, you can use this setting to increase the blink speed.

Screen savers

The Screen Saver option determines whether your monitor reverts to a screen-darkening display during periods of inactivity. This display helps prevent static screen objects, such as window title bars and menu bars, from "burning into" the monitor. You can choose from several animated displays, and you can set the period of inactivity after which the screen saver is turned on. If you have the IdleWild screen saver from the Windows Entertainment Pack, you can use its modules with this built-in screen saver. Simply copy all the module files (those ending with IW) and the IWLIB.DLL file into the WINDOWS directory.

Keyboard

In this Keyboard dialog box, you can set the rate at which keys repeat themselves when held down:

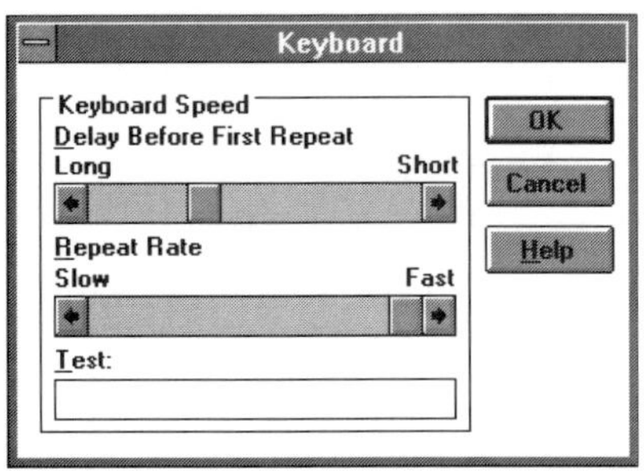

Key repeat speed

The Delay Before First Repeat scroll bar determines how long Windows waits before starting to repeat a key that is held down. You can select a delay from Long to Short. You can select a speed from Slow to Fast on the Repeat Rate scroll bar. To test the key repeat rate, click the Test box to position the insertion point, and hold down any character key. Then adjust the speed to suit your typing style.

Printers

Double-clicking the Printers icon opens this dialog box, which you probably saw when you first installed Windows and a printer:

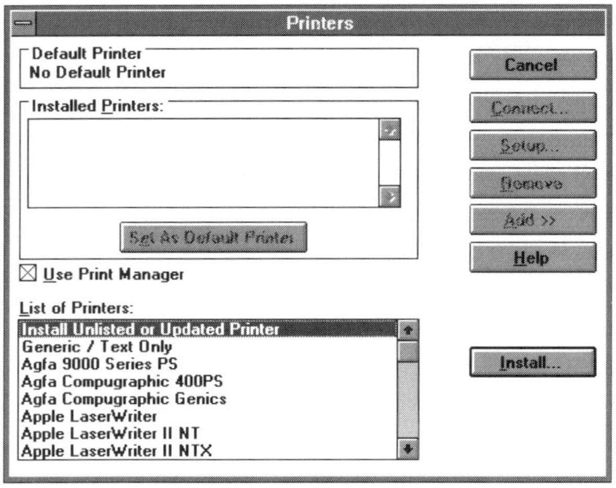

You can use the Printers dialog box to install another printer, remove a printer, set the default printer, and choose whether or not to use Print Manager. Buttons in the dialog box open other dialog boxes that allow you to configure a selected printer by specifying printer ports, paper size, source, orientation, and many other settings specific to your printer.

International

Double-clicking the International icon displays a dialog box in which you can select a country. Changing the country also changes settings such as the measurement system and date, time, currency, and number formats to reflect those used in that country:

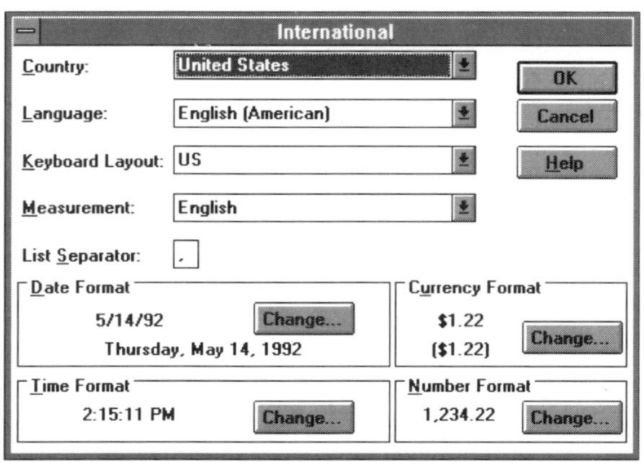

You can also change these settings individually.

Specifying language

In addition, you use the International option to specify the language you want to work in and the keyboard layout you want to use. Some Windows applications use the language setting for language-specific functions such as case conversion and sorting. The keyboard layout setting defines the special characters and symbols used by a language. Windows might ask you to insert some of your original installation disks when you change the International settings.

Date/Time

The Date/Time option sets the system date and time, just as the DOS Date and Time commands do. Simply select the number you want to change in this Date & Time dialog box:

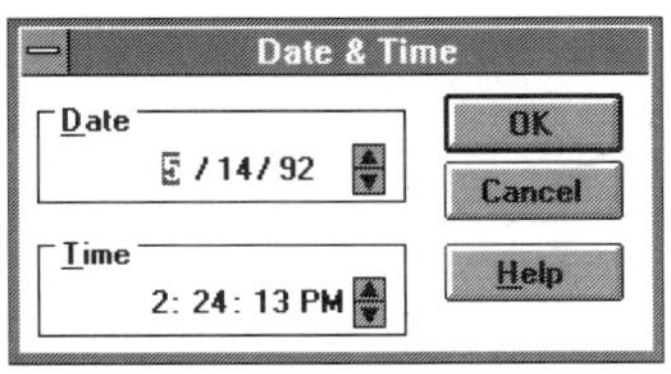

Then type a new number. You can also select the number and click the adjacent up and down arrows to change it. Note that the Date & Time dialog box reflects the date and time format set in the International dialog box.

386 Enhanced

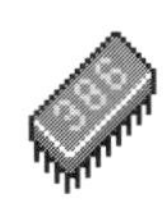

The 386 Enhanced option controls how Windows handles multitasking applications when running in 386 Enhanced mode and also sets up virtual-memory parameters. Double-clicking the option's icon displays this dialog box:

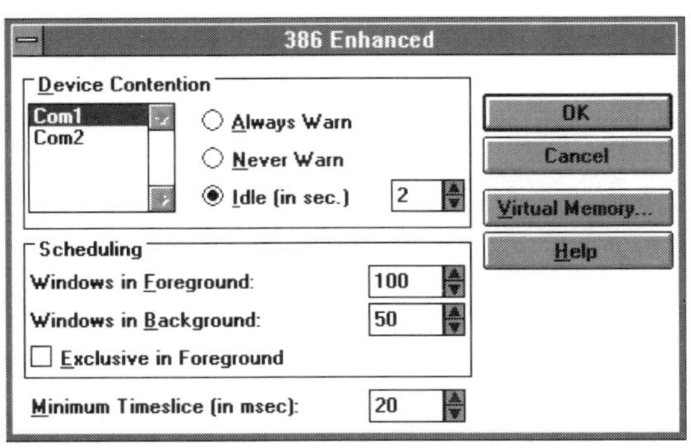

The Device Contention settings affect how Windows reacts when a multitasking non-Windows application and a Windows application attempt to access the same serial port. You can select between three options for each serial port on your computer: Always Warn, Never Warn, and the default, Idle.

The Scheduling and Minimum Timeslice settings both determine the processing time Windows devotes to each multitasking application. These settings, along with the Device Contention settings, are very technical and definitely not for the novice to play with. Microsoft recommends that you accept the default settings.

Virtual memory

Clicking the Virtual Memory button opens a dialog box that allows you to change the location, size, and type of swap file that Windows uses to create virtual memory on your hard disk. Having a large, permanent section of your hard disk set aside for a swap file greatly increases the speed at which Windows loads and runs on your machine. These options were first set when you installed Windows, and it is recommended that you accept the default settings. However, if you run into a crunch for hard-disk space, you can make a permanent swap file into a temporary one. Windows will then allocate as much free, contiguous hard-disk space as it can for a swap file each time you start Windows. If you find yourself running out of memory, even with a large, permanent swap file, you can change the size of the file using the New Size text box, which you access by clicking the Change button in the Virtual Memory dialog box.

Drivers

You use the Drivers option to install, remove, and configure drivers for devices such as sound cards, videodisc players, and MIDI sequencers. When you double-click the Drivers icon, this dialog box appears:

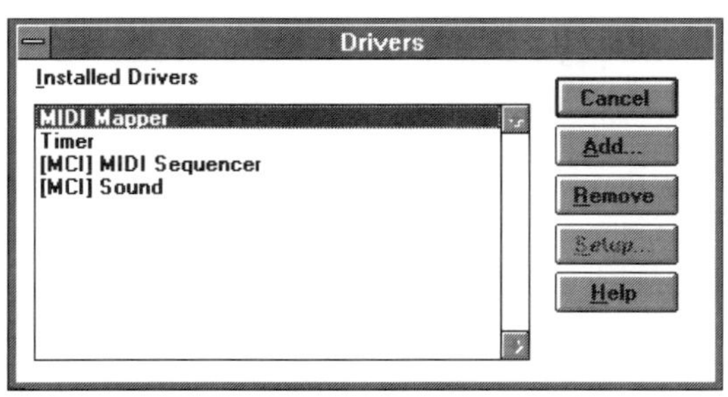

Even if a device is hooked up to your computer, Windows won't recognize it unless the proper driver is installed. Most devices come with appropriate drivers. Windows supplies several drivers for common sound devices. Click the Add button in the Drivers dialog box to see a list of available drivers.

Sound

If you have a sound card installed, you can use the Sound option to assign different sounds to system and application events in this dialog box:

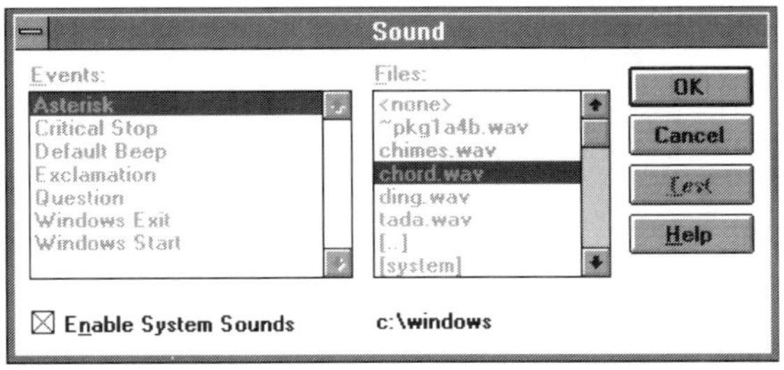

You can select a sound from among the several that come with Windows and then link it to a specific event, such as when you exit Windows or when a warning dialog box appears. If you don't have a sound card installed, all the choices in the Sound dialog box are unavailable, except for Enable System Sounds. (This choice simply toggles the standard system warning beep on and off.)

Network

If you are working on a network, the Network icon appears in the Control Panel window. Double-clicking this icon displays the Network window.

Because there are many different types of networks, generalizing about them can be difficult. Check with your network system administrator for procedures that are specific to your network. In this section, we discuss basic procedures that will work on most types of networks.

Logging on

Logging on to a network usually involves entering a user name and password each time you need to access the network. Generic steps for logging on are given on the next page.

1. Double-click the Network icon to open the Network window.
2. Choose Logon from the Account menu to display the Logon dialog box.
3. Type your user name in the Username text box. If your network requires that you enter a logon password, type the password in the Password text box.
4. Click Logon. You can now use all the network resources available to you.

All networks are different, and logon procedures and restrictions differ for each. If you see a warning message indicating a network error, contact your network system administrator.

Logging off

After you have finished using the network, you need to log off. Some users simply turn off their computers without logging off, but logging off allows the network to disconnect gracefully and alerts any users who are accessing your machine. To log off:

1. Open Control Panel in Program Manager, and double-click the Network icon.
2. Choose the Logoff command from the Account menu. You will be disconnected from the network and will no longer be able to use network applications. If you are using a copy of Windows that you installed from the network server, you should now exit Windows.
3. Close the Network window, close the Control Panel, and choose Exit Windows from Program Manager's File menu to quit Windows.

Network tips

When you are using Windows on a network, keep in mind the following:

- Always start the network software before you start Windows. Usually, the network software must load as memory-resident before Windows loads. If you load Windows first, the network software may interfere with the way Windows handles memory.
- When creating icons in Program Manager for applications and documents that are stored on the network server,

always preface the file location with the appropriate server drive letter.

- You don't have to create Program Manager icons to run network programs. You can use File Manager or the Run command to start them.

Windows may behave differently on some networks than on others. If you are having difficulties, consult the Windows documentation or your network system administrator.

Windows Setup

You use Windows Setup to change the equipment settings you made (or Setup made) when you first installed Windows. For example, if you change your monitor, keyboard, mouse, or network software after you have installed Windows, you need to tell Windows about the change. Double-click the Windows Setup icon to open this window:

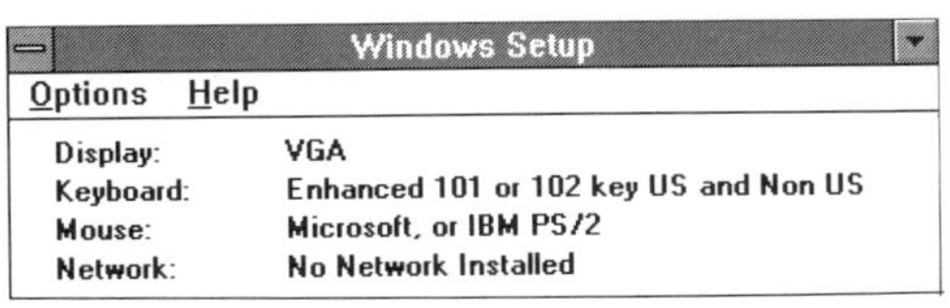

You can then choose Change System Settings from the Options menu. Select new settings as appropriate from the Display, Keyboard, Mouse, and Network drop-down lists, and insert any disks Windows prompts you for.

Installing program icons

You can also use Windows Setup to install program icons in Program Manager. For example, suppose you acquire a disk full of public-domain utilities and want to create icons for them. Copy the files to a directory on your path, and choose the Set Up Applications command from the Options menu. In the Setup Applications dialog box, you can indicate whether you want Windows Setup to search for applications or ask you to specify an application. If you want to specify an application, follow the same procedures for adding an icon to Program Manager that we described in Chapter 2. If you want to search for an application, Windows Setup lists all applications it recognizes on the selected drive, including some for which you probably already have icons. (Follow the instructions on the screen.) Select the programs that need icons, click Add, and then click OK. Setup creates the icons, putting them in the Applications group window. If Windows doesn't recognize a non-Windows application, you'll need to create a PIF file for it (see page 106).

Adding and removing Windows components

If disk space was tight when you installed Windows, you might not have installed a Windows file that you now need. Or you might have installed them all and now want to jettison some of them because space is getting tight. Either way, you use the Add/Remove Windows Components command on the Options menu. The categories you can add or remove are Readme Files, Accessories (which includes almost all of the Windows tools), Games, Screen Savers, and Wallpapers Misc. Select a category by putting an X in the adjacent check box. Click the Files button next to the category if you want to select individual files within the category. If you're adding files, be ready to insert disks as Setup asks for them.

System Configuration Editor

Editing system files

Windows 3.1 comes with an undocumented but very useful tool called System Configuration Editor, which is a simple text editor that automatically opens four of your system's most important configuration files: AUTOEXEC.BAT, CONFIG.SYS, SYSTEM.INI, and WIN.INI. You're probably familiar with AUTOEXEC.BAT and CONFIG.SYS, which affect your entire system's performance and carry out functions such as turning on extended memory managers and mouse drivers and setting the path for directories. SYSTEM.INI and WIN.INI perform similar functions, but affect only Windows. These files record default settings for programs, tell Windows where to look for particular files, and so forth. Many Windows programs add instructions to these files when you first install or run them.

The System Configuration Editor program is tucked away in the WINDOWS\SYSTEM subdirectory under the filename SYSEDIT.EXE. To start the program, simply double-click its filename in File Manager. (You can also create an icon for it or use the Run command on File Manager's File menu.)

The System Configuration Editor window looks something like this:

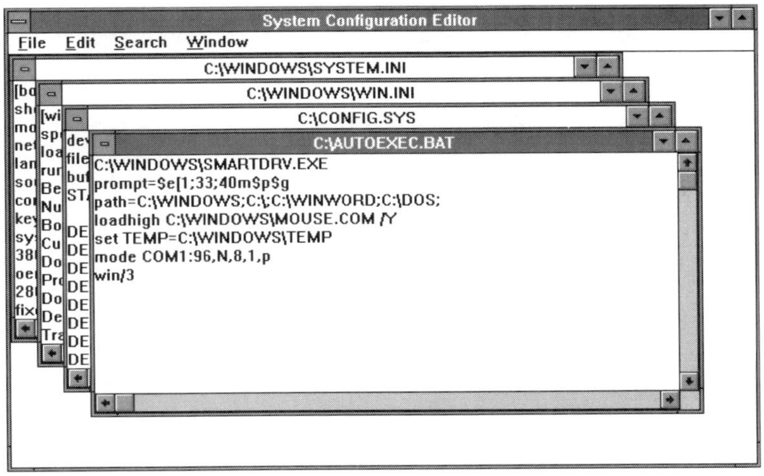

In this window, you can edit the configuration files just like Notepad text files. Having made all the necessary changes, choose Save from the File menu to save the new version of the file. (If you choose Exit from the File menu, System Configuration Editor prompts you to save your changes.)

A word of warning: A mistake in any of these files can have serious consequences. Always back up the original files on a bootable disk before making changes so that you can restore the unedited version if necessary.

Appendix
Notes About Installation

Windows Setup, the Windows installation program, guides you painlessly through the entire process of getting the program onto your computer. Windows Setup also customizes Windows for your specific computer configuration. If Windows is not yet installed on your system, read this appendix to be sure that you have the right equipment and that you know the answers to the questions Windows Setup will ask.

Necessary Equipment

You need several basic pieces of equipment to run Windows. Here is an overview of what you should have.

Type of Computer

You can run Windows on a computer with the Intel 80286 chip, such as the IBM AT and PS/2 or compatibles, but you might not be satisfied with the results because many Windows' features, including multitasking of non-Windows applications, will be unavailable. To take full advantage of Windows, you need a computer with a 386 or 486 chip.

Amount of Memory

Your computer must have at least 640 KB of standard memory plus 256 KB of extended memory for Standard mode, and 640 KB of standard memory plus 1024 KB of extended memory for 386 Enhanced mode. Keep in mind that these figures are the minimum amount of memory required. The more memory you have, the better. All memory beyond 640 KB should be configured as extended memory. If you are uncertain of your computer's memory configuration, check your computer or your computer or memory-board documentation, or call your dealer. If you have MS-DOS version 5 installed, use the MEM command at the command line to find out how your computer's memory is configured. You can also find public domain utilities on public and commercial bulletin boards that report on your computer's configuration.

Some extended memory managers are incompatible with the Windows memory manager. If you are running an incompatible memory manager, Windows Setup displays a dialog box asking whether you want to disable your extended memory manager. You probably want to answer Yes. You can always re-enable the memory manager later if disabling it causes problems with other software, or you can keep separate AUTOEXEC.BAT and CONFIG.SYS files for different work situations.

Operating System

You should be running MS-DOS or PC-DOS version 3.1 or later. If you have an earlier version of either DOS, you will have to upgrade to a newer version. We strongly recommend using MS-DOS version 5, which has many features that will help you free up precious memory.

Disk Drives

You need a hard-disk drive with 6 to 8 MB of free storage space, and a high-density floppy-disk drive (for transferring programs from the installation disks). If you plan on running Windows in 386 Enhanced mode, you will also need to set aside as much free disk space as possible for a swap file, which Windows uses to create virtual memory. To find out how much free space is on your hard drive, type *dir* (for *directory*) at the DOS prompt, and press Enter. After listing the files and subdirectories in the active directory, DOS tells you how many bytes of disk space are free on the active drive.

Type of Display

Windows can work with many different monitors and graphics display adapters, but the graphical interface really comes into its own with a color VGA or Super VGA display. If you do a Custom Setup installation, Windows Setup can provide a list of the display devices for which Windows has driver programs. If your display is not on the list, you can select a generic display driver—one that works with many types of displays—or you can consult your display manufacturer to see whether a driver has been developed specifically for your display and Windows.

Mouse

In theory, you can use Windows without a mouse, but as far as we are concerned, a mouse is not optional equipment because using Windows from the keyboard is so cumbersome. If you don't have a mouse, you should buy one. Most mice come with either two or three buttons, but the second button rarely gets used, and we've never found a use for a third one. Windows supports several different types of mice. If you do a Custom Setup installation, Windows Setup can provide a list of the mice for which Windows has driver programs. If your mouse is not on the list, you can select a generic mouse driver—one that works with many types of mice—or you can consult your mouse manufacturer to see whether a driver has been developed specifically for your mouse and Windows.

Optional Windows Applications

To get the maximum benefit from the Windows environment, you should use applications written specifically for Windows, such as Microsoft Word, Microsoft Excel, WordPerfect, Ami Pro, Lotus 1-2-3, Aldus PageMaker, Corel Draw, and others. Many software companies have written Windows versions of their most popular software.

Optional Equipment

To use the Windows telecommunications program, Terminal, you need a modem. And to print your files, you need a printer. Windows supports many different types of printers. If your printer is not on Windows Setup's list of supported devices, call your printer manufacturer to see whether a driver has been developed specifically for your printer and Windows. Windows 3.1 also has built-in support for many different multimedia devices, like sound cards, MIDI sequencers, CD-ROM, and audio CD players.

What Windows Setup Needs to Know

If you select the Express Setup option when you run Windows Setup, the program analyzes your computer's hardware and system software and attempts to configure Windows to best suit your current setup. You can usually rely on Windows Setup to correctly configure Windows throughout the installation procedure.

If you select the Custom Setup option, you will need to give Windows Setup the following information:

- The directory to which it will copy the Windows programs. By default, Setup creates a WINDOWS directory on your C drive. If you want, you can specify a different directory and a different drive. Throughout this book, we assume you are running Windows from this directory.
- The type of computer you have.
- The type of monitor you have.
- The type of mouse you have—if any.
- The type of keyboard you have—standard or extended.
- The language you want to work in.
- The type of network you have—if any.
- The type of printer you have—if any—and what port it is connected to.

If you change your printer or any other piece of equipment after installing Windows, you can run the Windows Setup program from within Windows to update the installation information.

Running Windows Setup

Installation with Windows Setup is really just a matter of reading the instructions at the bottom of each Setup screen and responding to prompts for disks. Pressing Enter at each step of the installation procedure accepts the defaults. If you are unsure about a procedure while running Windows Setup, press F1 for additional help. To start Windows Setup:

1. Insert Disk 1 into your floppy drive. (We assume from now on that your floppy drive is drive A.)
2. At the C prompt, type *A:\SETUP*, and press Enter. An introductory screen appears with three options:
   - To learn more about Windows Setup before continuing, press F1.
   - To set up Windows now, press Enter.
   - To quit the Windows Setup program without installing Windows, press F3.
3. Windows Setup then gives you the choice of Express Setup or Custom Setup. Express Setup is recommended because it automates the process. Use Custom Setup if you think you will be using different hardware than is currently installed, such as a different monitor or keyboard. Press Enter for Express Setup, or C for Custom Setup.
4. If you selected Custom Setup, Windows Setup asks where you want the program installed. If Windows Setup finds an older version of Windows, it asks whether you want to update it. Press Enter to accept the defaults, or type a new directory name, and press Enter.

   Windows Setup then begins copying files to your hard drive. Insert disks when prompted. Halfway through the installation process, Windows Setup will have copied enough of the Windows graphical environment files to your hard drive to continue the procedure from within Windows itself. You can tell when the switch to Windows occurs, because Windows Setup starts displaying dialog boxes with three-dimensional buttons. The Windows Setup dialog box displays the name of the file currently being copied and gives you an idea of how much of the installation process has been carried out. Although Windows Setup is now running in Windows, you can still accept its defaults by pressing Enter or by clicking the Continue button.

5. Windows Setup then asks you to personalize the program with your name and your company name. Type in this information, and press Enter. Windows Setup asks you to verify the information you typed. If everything is correct, press Enter again.

6. Windows Setup then asks if you want to install a printer driver. Select a printer driver, and press Enter. You can worry about configuring the printer later.

   Toward the end of the installation process, Windows Setup searches your hard drive for Windows applications, creates icons for them, and puts them in a set of windows.

7. When Windows Setup is finished, you can run a Windows tutorial, or you can skip it.

8. Next, Windows Setup displays a dialog box telling you that it has successfully installed Windows. Because Windows Setup might have altered your AUTOEXEC.BAT and CONFIG.SYS files, it's a good idea to reboot your computer. Click the Return To MS-DOS button, and then reboot your computer by pressing Ctrl+Alt+Del.

   While Windows Setup is running, you can press the F3 key to exit the program. However, we don't recommend that you interrupt the program in this way, even if you give the wrong information, because Windows will not be properly installed, and you will have to remove all the installed files and run the Windows Setup program again. You are better off allowing the program to completely install Windows and then running Windows Setup again from within Windows to correct any mistakes.

   If your computer crashes during the Setup process, irreparable harm may have been done to the Windows files already on your hard disk. Delete all the files in the WINDOWS directory, and run Windows Setup again.

Index

W

About the Authors

Salley Oberlin
Having started her computer-book publishing career at Sybex, in 1983 Oberlin moved to Seattle, WA, to become one of the founding directors of Microsoft Press. Co-owner of Online Press, she has been a major force in putting high-quality computer books on the bookstore shelves.

Patrick Kervran
A writer and technical editor with a flare for simple explanations and straightforward instructions, Kervran is coauthor of *A Quick Course™ in Excel for Windows* and *A Quick Course™ in Lotus 1-2-3 for Windows*. He lives in Seattle, WA.

Joyce Cox
With 12 years experience in writing and editing, Cox has specialized in making technical subjects accessible to non-technical audiences. She is the coauthor of five *Quick Course™* titles. Before cofounding Online Press, Cox was Managing Editor of Microsoft Press.

About Online Press

Founded in 1986, Online Press is a group of publishing professionals working to make the presentation and access of information manageable, efficient, accurate, and economical. In 1991, we began publishing our popular *Quick Course™* computer-book series, which offers streamlined instruction for the busy professional. At Online Press, it is our goal to help computer users quickly learn what they need to know about today's most popular software programs to get their work done efficiently.

Acknowledgments

Many thanks to Christy Gersich at Microsoft; Peter Mayfield and the gang at CityRock Gym; and to Randy Fleming, Mark Ouimet, and the rest of the team at Publishers Group West.

Cover design and photography by Tom Draper Design
Interior text design by Joyce Cox and Salley Oberlin
Graphics by Polly Urban
Layout by Bill Teel
Proofreading by Christina Smith
Printed by Viking Press Inc.
Otabind® cover by Muscle Bound Bindery

Text composition by Online Press in Times Roman, with display type in Avant Garde Gothic Bold, using Ventura Publisher and the Linotronic 300 laser imagesetter.

Other *Quick Course*™ Books

Don't miss the other titles in our *Quick Course*™ series! Quality books at the unbeatable price of $12.95.

- *A Quick Course in Word 2.0 for Windows*
- *A Quick Course in Excel 4 for Windows*
- *A Quick Course in WordPerfect for Windows*
- *A Quick Course in Lotus 1-2-3 for Windows*
- *A Quick Course in WordPerfect 5.1*
- *A Quick Course in DOS 5*
- *A Quick Course in Lotus 1-2-3, version 2.4* (Summer 1992)
- *A Quick Course in Paradox for Windows* (Summer 1992)

Plus more to come...

For our latest catalog, call (800) 854-3344 or write to us at:

In the U.S., *Quick Course*™ books are $12.95 each. You'll find them in bookstores and computer stores, or check with us at Online Press at 14320 NE 21st Street, Suite 18, Bellevue, Washington 98007 (206-641-3434 or 800-854-3344).

Quick Course™ books are distributed to bookstores in the U.S. by *Publishers Group West*, Emeryville, CA (510-658-3453 or 800-788-3123) and by *major wholesalers*; in Australia by *Step Up Systems* (03-427-0168); and in the United Kingdom by *Computer Bookshops Ltd.* (021-706-1188).